THE LOVELINESS PROJECT

THE PATH TO MY PURPOSE

Visionary Author: Tatiana Tinsley Dorsey

Visionary Author: T'Keyah Gray

Foreword Author: Diamonique Valentine

Expert Author: Kiara Anthony

Expert Author: Kelsey Armstrong

Book Cover Design: Little Publishing LLC

Published By: Little Publishing LLC

ISBN: 978-1-7343314-8-6

Founder's Message

Tatiana Tinsley Dorsey & T'Keyah Gray

In the inspiring words of Oprah Winfrey, "Follow your passion. It will lead you to your purpose." Our passion? Empowering Black women, across all generations, to live their life with purpose, on purpose. We already know that Black women, at any age and stage in their life, are capable of doing it all. We also know that, more often than not, society frequently aims to silence our stories and our voices in ways that diminish our experiences. Black women are rarely provided with the safe space to be vulnerable. We are often perceived to possess, and we are forced into a perimeter of super strength. That is truly an unfair burden for us to carry.

Ten years ago, at the start of our journey, our team set out to make an impact in the lives of younger women with a specific focus of marginalized communities. We formed to create experiences where younger women could feel empowered by our mission to build, uplift and guide our sisters through their life transitions in the form of mentorship. Our journey created an organization titled, *The LadyBUGS,* that aims to empower younger Black women to take their magic and make their mark on the world. In completing this mission, we have worked to provide opportunities for their talents to be showcased and assist in preparing for their future. As we continued on our journey, we learned that we were missing the opportunity to cultivate a community of women that had the most impactful contribution to our mentored population. Therefore, the partnership of *The LadyBUGS* and our LLC, *The Loveliness Network,* began. This partnership assists in providing resources to our community of focus, supports causes that affect Black women, and offers resources to support them in their academic endeavors.

The Loveliness Network, LLC is our dedicated platform with the sole purpose to connect the experiences of Black women showcasing their stories by elevating and empowering their voices. A common explanation of loveliness defines the word with the meaning of beauty and attractiveness. But, by second definition, it also means a large group of ladybugs. This group of ladybugs is so enormous that it is often picked up by weather systems as a force of nature. Imagine the disturbance in the atmosphere when Black women collectively come together to enlighten the world by sharing their experiences that often go unheard. We present to you: *The Loveliness Project.*

As Dr. Maya Angelou once said, "There is no greater agony than bearing an untold story inside of you." The Loveliness Project aims to alleviate that agony in our dedicated space of storytelling through various topics of interest in the form of a book series collaboration. The purpose of this book, our inaugural edition, is to present a lovely collection of stories focusing on the topic of The Path to My Purpose.

In this book, we share stories told by Black women—not only in celebration of their successes—but also to highlight the obstacles they have overcome and the magic it took to get there. Our objective in this project is to enlighten our community by sharing our stories. When the world attempts to silence our voices, one elevated voice can be the catalyst of empowering another. The empowerment of multiple voices can create an unstoppable series that is unable to impede our ability to excel together. There are so many instances where we witness our voices being suppressed and our stories surpassed.

That ends here.

We would like to extend a special thank you to our foreword author, Diamonique Valentine, whose story of strength and resilience highlights the beauty of her transformation and survival. To our amazing expert authors, we thank you for your unwavering commitment and dedication to this project. To our phenomenal contributing authors, thank you for trusting us with your stories, and thank you for your vulnerability and willingness to share your magic with the world. To our partners and sponsors, thank you for your contribution to this effort and devotedness in elevating the voices of Black women.

Our message to our readers:

Hey Lovely,

Our entire reason for creating *The Loveliness Network, LLC* is to lift up our voices, share our stories and make sure the world fully sees us—our struggles, our triumphs and everything in between. As we have matriculated through life, met new people, and experienced new places and cultures, we are always left in astonishment of Black women. Everything about us is amazing. Our magic is unmatched, and more often than not, the diamond-like sparkle seen shining from us was created from surviving enormous amounts of pressure, always persevering with the utmost poise and brilliance.

To us, this project is more than sharing the richness of our experiences. This is our effort in joining the forces of others with similar missions, in capturing the lightning in a bottle that is the epitome of the Black woman. Our hope is to not only celebrate the strength of Black women, and the beauty in our stories, but also to provide the safe space to be vulnerable. Our openness will not only inspire other women in similar circumstances. It will also bring awareness to the trials we face.

Remember to value your self-worth, love who you are, and know that you have been placed on this earth for a divine purpose, on purpose. A purpose that can never be duplicated. There is only one individual creation of you! We will shine in this thing called life together. The Loveliness Network has been created to take your journey with you and serve as a place where you realize that some of the hills and valleys you have faced in life have not only created you into the beautiful being that you are but has also impacted other women similar to you.

As our network continues to grow, we plan to learn from and support each other through our achievements and obstacles. Our promise to you is to continue providing this space: one where we can collectively *empower, elevate, enlighten, explore and excel.* Thank you for your interest and investment in our stories.

Your purchase of this book not only supports the goals of *The Loveliness Network,* but also positively impacts the resources of *The LadyBUGS* community.

Be sure to stay connected with us and join our network via our website, thelovelinessnetwork.com; Podcast: Hey Lovely; and social media channels: Instagram and Facebook @ TheLovelinessNetwork.

About Tatiana Tinsley Dorsey

Tatiana graduated from North Carolina Agricultural & Technical State University in 2011 with a Bachelor of Arts degree in Psychology, she later pursued a Master's Degree in Human Resources Management graduating in 2014.

Currently residing in The Greater Atlanta Area, Tatiana works in the Consumer Goods Industry in the space of Diversity, Equity, and Inclusion. She is dedicated to creating inclusive and equitable working environments where employees feel welcomed and bring their "whole-selves" to work, and having the opportunity to grow, contribute and develop.

She continues her commitment of community service within her ownership and operation of The LadyBUGS, a 501c(3) mentoring organization with a mission to Build, Uplift and Guide our Sisters. Her org is committed to ensuring every girl is empowered, specifically targeting those of marginalized groups.

Personally, Tatiana is married to her college sweetheart, Donald Dorsey. The two are proud parents of a very active toddler, Dillon Blake (and a fur baby Bella).

About T'Keyah Gray

T'Keyah Gray is an accomplished human resources professional with a knack for talent and recruitment. She is a graduate of the North Carolina Agricultural & Technical State University where she earned a bachelor's degree in Psychology in 2014. She went on to obtain a master's degree in Human Resources Management in 2016 from the University of Maryland Global Campus.

T'Keyah currently serves in the federal government as a Human Resources professional, specializing in recruitment, staffing and procedures. Personally, she is an active member of Zeta Phi Beta Sorority, Incorporated devoted to the principles of Scholarship, Service, Sisterhood and Finer Womanhood. She continues to follow her commitment to community service within her dedication to The LadyBUGS, a 501c(3) mentoring organization committed to ensuring every girl is empowered and works to empower others. Most recently, she co-founded The Loveliness Network LLC, a dedicated platform focused on elevating the voices of Black women through storytelling.

Contents

Foreword

Diamonique Valentine

The voices and stories of African American women have been silenced since slavery, when silence was necessary for survival. If a Black woman broke her silence about abuse, there was no justice. Instead, there was punishment and consequences for speaking out about the abuse. We were not seen as human, nor did we deserve protection. We were labeled as promiscuous and forced to believe that we were deserving of our traumas. This created a code of silence and a lack of storytelling. I know you may be thinking, "That was over 400 years ago." But the silent treatment that once was accepted for survival is very much still prevalent in today's society. This book aims to connect the experiences of African American women through their powerful voices and stories.

Many of us have shared experiences where we have felt silenced. Some of us have felt silenced through systematic racism, in areas like the criminal justice system, employment, the wealth gap, education, housing, health care disparities and abuse. We have felt discrimination in the workplace. We have been neglected in our communities and even silenced in our homes. Feel empowered by the brave voices in this book. Be inspired by how African American women are breaking the silence that we all experience through collective storytelling. These featured authors have found their purpose and have overcome many obstacles. Let these life-changing experiences from each author inspire you to do the same.

My heart is full of love for the founders of The Loveliness Project, who created a space for women like us to share our stories filled with various topics of interest. The Loveliness Network, LLC partners with The LadyBUGS, a 501(c)(3) nonprofit organization that aims to elevate the stories of Black women of all generations, providing resources to bridge the gap through life transitions.

I want to personally thank you ladies for hearing my voice as an

African American woman who was diagnosed with stage three triple negative breast cancer at the age of twenty-seven. Triple negative breast cancer is an aggressive form of breast cancer that predominantly affects young women and African American women. The median age of breast cancer diagnoses is sixty-two. I was shocked, overwhelmed, afraid, worried, confused and deeply saddened by my diagnoscs. I was told to write my will at the age of twenty-seven. I was hurt, but I wanted to live. So, I knew I had to fight.

"I am lucky that whatever fear I have inside of me, my desire to win is always stronger." *Serena Williams.*

I was the person who could solve every problem and turn every bad situation upside down, but I had no answer for this. My life changed overnight. Before I heard the words, "You have cancer," I felt like I was this "strong" woman. Suddenly, I felt weird when people heard my story and messaged me, "You're so strong." I realized I didn't want that label anymore. I realized I was a real life human, going through a life and death matter. *Strong* was the last thing I wanted to be. I didn't choose strong, and I realized that being strong was unrealistic. I wasn't strong. I was terrified for my life. I was scared to be in pain, scared of what the chemo would do to my body. I was worried about the chemo not working and worried about the cancer spreading. I was shaken about being sick and now looking sick. I was worried that I would lack intimacy with my husband, fearful at the thought of treatment destroying my ability to have children. I was afraid of damaging my body while trying to heal this cancer. I panicked at the thought of trying to maintain my life and business. I was anxious about the year I would spend in treatment, and all the events I would miss due to my immune system being compromised. Sad at the thought of not being around my family and friends, I was completely traumatized by all the surgeries and testing I would undergo. I wasn't strong. I was trying to *survive.* With hope, God, my husband, family, community, doctors and nurses at the cancer center, a lot of crying, breakdowns and appointments with the health social worker, I made it through. I want every woman to know that it's okay and it's safe to take that strong label off.

I used my traumatic, life-changing diagnosis to connect with women who were also fighting battles. I realized a lot of women were fighting in silence. Many were fighting alone. My goal was to show that a diagnosis is not an automatic death sentence. Tragedy sometimes has a weird way of showing you how much you matter and how much you are genuinely loved. Through my journey and storytelling, I felt an overwhelming amount of love—not only from my husband, my family, my friends and my community—but also from strangers. My story has not only saved lives through early detection, but freely sharing was an outlet my spirit needed. I can't imagine what would have happened if I put the silent treatment to my story due to shame and fear. Millions of people shared my story and prayed for me. I felt those prayers daily. I deserved to live. Everyone's battle may not look like sixteen rounds of an aggressive chemotherapy treatment and a double mastectomy. However, the burden of your storm may feel just as heavy. Although others may see you as *strong*, I see you as a *survivor.*

My life's purpose is to show the beauty in the chaos. Being alive is proof that God still has a glorious purpose for your life. I was attacked in one of the areas that I took pride in: my health. At the age of twenty-two, I became a health and wellness entrepreneur. I took pride in my healthy active lifestyle and my work of empowering clients all over the country to live a healthy lifestyle through nutrition and fitness. Then, I got cancer and it stung me to my core. I felt robbed. Robbed of my passion, my career, my life. But even through my storm, women continuously sought my help and guidance. Fear wanted me to believe I wasn't qualified. But love showed me that I was even more qualified because I now have more knowledge and wisdom through experiences that have shaken me physically and mentally. Knowing that God was with me in the midst of my storm gave me an assurance that I was going to be alright. I knew I would live. Life's uncertainties can sometimes take unexpected turns. But it cannot take your faith, your hope, your joy, your peace, your purpose. It cannot destroy love and it cannot take your life.

Weeping may endure for a night, but joy comes in the morning.

Turn the page. Be inspired by the authors who graciously poured their love and stories through these pages.

About Diamonique Valentine

Growing up Diamonique Valentine considered herself to the queen of Extracurriculars activities. She was always seeking opportunities and searching her purpose at a young age. As a student athlete, she attended The University of the District of Columbia and graduated with her bachelor's degree in 2015. Her senior year in college, her spark in the Health & Wellness industry. Diamonique's excitement, results and passion started her part time business at the age of 22 years old, while giving her vision for what she could create for herself as a full-time entrepreneur.

Today, along with her husband, they are known for coaching and guiding clients from all over the country on their healthy active lifestyle journey. Under their umbrella of work, they have held massive fitness classes and also opened a healthy shake and tea bar in Diamonique's hometown, Camden, NJ.

After being diagnosed with triple negative breast cancer, they decided to take their business 100% online, so she could heal while working from home. The gratitude she has for entrepreneurship was magnified during tough seasons. She enjoys her time, freedom, and the ability to be flexible with her work and her passion.

Sharing her journey of conquering breast cancer while living a healthy, happy, and whole life, her story reached and inspired millions of people online. This experience gave her the opportunity to inspire and impact lives at another level. As a thriver and survivor, she has been featured in magazines, news segments, health events gearing to disparities in the African American community, speaking to colleges, organizations around the world for prevention and early detection and even had the opportunity to share her story on Ellen The Show.

Outside of her business she enjoys traveling, creating memories with her husband and spending time with her family.

Defining the Spark

Kelsey Armstrong

Purpose. It's a word that sometimes can be scary to think about. When do you know that you are fulfilling your purpose? What if you don't know your purpose? Society has created a façade that, as young adults, we need to know what we want to do, when we will do it, and how. But this is nowhere close to reality. One way I have personally tried to understand my purpose is through my faith. I have thought numerous times that I was going to do one thing. However, God has a funny way of working things out. You may think that you are going in one direction, but He aligns things that will lead you differently. Learning from this fact, I have found what my purpose is, though I have fought and ran away from it many times. However, lately, especially during the pandemic, I have learned to listen to God and to follow the purpose He has laid out for me. It gives me the spark and twinkle in my eyes, even when I don't want to admit it. However, being stubborn, I have to discover and accept my spark.

As a child, I absolutely hated school. However, I excelled in it. I had A's and B's throughout middle school, high school and undergrad. I struggled at first when I started my master's program, which was a humbling experience in itself. But once I got the help I needed, I continued to make good grades. After completing my master's degree, I said I was done with school and academia. But as graduation came and left, and I moved from New York back to North Carolina, I received a big piece of humble pie. I could not find a job in journalism, mass communication and public relations. Facing that I had a master's degree with no job made me feel defeated. I felt like all the schooling I completed was for nothing. It made me ultimately question my purpose.

In an effort to make some type of coin, I became a substitute teacher. Mind you, once I finished my master's, I told myself I was done with academia in all forms. However, there I found myself back in a classroom as a substitute. I enjoyed subbing for teachers and developed relationships where I was working every day. From these relationships, I was told about a permanent job at an elementary school: a kindergarten teacher's assistant. I interviewed and accepted the job. There again, I found myself back in the classroom, helping others and being creative in developing and executing lesson plans.

One day, as I was recovering from the flu, I received a message from the lead teacher that he was not going to be in the classroom for an extended period of time. He hadn't created any lesson plans. Still recovering from the flu, I went into the classroom the next day. I went from a teacher's assistant to a lead teacher. As I was teaching, I felt a spark, and even the assistant principal let me know that I had a spark when teaching. She told me that I needed to either become a teacher or further my education by pursuing a doctoral degree. I could see myself doing so in the back of mind, but I did not want to admit it.

Shortly after this experience, I received an opportunity to work at my alma mater, the illustrious North Carolina Agricultural and Technical State University, as a communications specialist. Thinking that I had now started my career, I still thought, How did I find myself yet back at school? The first year in the position was rough, as I did not have much freedom to be creative when developing content strategies or designing social media graphics. I discovered that I breathe creativity. When it is shut off, I am unfulfilled. Since I felt like my job was at a dead end, I continued to look for other job opportunities. However, I never went beyond the interview phase. God kept me at this job for a reason, but I did not want to stay.

In 2019, I decided to apply for my Ph.D. I couldn't believe I was going back to school. I thought of the old assistant principal. I had run from academia so much, but I finally gave in and accepted that pursuing a Ph.D. would allow me to learn and become better in my craft. However, when it came to my job, I was still there. The year 2018 came and left, and 2019 came and left. I was still at the job. In 2020, the pandemic changed everything. I was able to blossom. My creativity was able to be used, and I was able to shine. By being able to shine, I found that I could use my communications, content strategy, social media and other communications elements to help others. The thought of combining creativity, academia, communications, and helping people by finding creative ways to conveying messaging that would ultimately benefit them made the spark ignite. As I continued my doctoral program, I found that what I was learning could also be applied to what ignited my spark. I also found where the needs for effective communications were.

It is not always easy. Plan A still doesn't always work. But, hey, you still have the rest of the alphabet to create plans. But through the struggle and overcoming challenges, and being stubborn, I have discovered my spark: helping others through developing creative, innovative ways to convey messages in higher education. I know my spark continues to kindle as I discover more about myself and my craft.

About Kelsey Armstrong

Kelsey A. Armstrong is a southern bell from North Carolina. Kelsey received her bachelor's degree in Journalism and Mass Communication with a concentration in broadcast production from North Carolina A&T State University and her master's degree in public relations from Syracuse University. She is currently pursuing her doctorate in communications from Liberty University. She is currently a communications specialist for Cooperative Extension at N.C. A&T with expertise in social media management, analytics, strategy, and content creation. In her free time, she loves crafting, dancing, and true-crime TV.

Kelsey is committed to community service, dedicating her time and communications know-how as the Chief Marketing Officer to The LadyBUGS, a 501c(3) mentoring organization committed to ensuring every girl is empowered and works to empower others. She also serves in the same role with The Loveliness Network LLC, a dedicated platform focused on elevating the voices of Black women through storytelling.

It's Okay to Be Clueless

Kiara Anthony

Purpose.

There have been a few instances where someone's asked me about purpose.

"Do you know what your purpose is?"

"What's your why?"

"Where do you feel God is leading you to?"

By a show of hands, who knows what their purpose is?

In case you're wondering, my hand is lying flat on the table.

Do I know what my purpose is? The true answer? I have no f*cking clue.

I've navigated through life by doing all the right things. I graduated high school and went on to college. Excelled at it. Got accepted into a master's program without issue. Finished with honors. I even landed a job right after school. From the outside looking in, you could say I'm successful. And maybe I am. But it never felt like it was ever enough.

Growing up, I'd always been the youngest or the annoying tagalong. I always felt like I had to compete for the attention of my brothers or my family. I had to keep up with my friends because they always seemed to be three steps ahead of me. I needed to be liked by my supervisors and coworkers to stay relevant. I didn't want to be left behind. I needed — I craved — to be front and center to feel validated that my success and my achievements were enough.

Have you ever been complimented on something, and you respond with, "Thanks, but…"? Or maybe you downplay your achievements by explaining how ordinary it was to get to where you are. Well...that was me. In fact, that had always been me. Back then, purpose meant successfully keeping up with everyone else...and making sure they all saw it. My journey meant nothing if it wasn't at the same caliber of my friends or at the notion of being "more ahead for my age." But we all know that's a recipe for disaster, depression and disappointment. And believe me when I say I've experienced all three.

I know my story — a short one, at that — is one many of us share. To feel like we're never doing enough or that there's always just "one more thing" for us to do before we can be content with where we are. We navigate through life as if there's a roadmap to true purpose or happiness. We live every day just to make it to the next one, rather than taking a moment to celebrate ourselves and acknowledge how far we've come.

Which brings me to the purpose (see what I did there) of this project. We all have a unique story to tell. It's our responsibility to share it, inspire others and celebrate our greatness. Purpose is a journey. Though it may seem insignificant to you, your story could be the answer someone else is looking for.

When asked to be a part of The Loveliness Project, my initial thought was, "Wow! I get to join a collection of badass women who've achieved and overcome so much. But what am I going to share? Better yet, who am I to share?" (See...there's that doubt and validation peeking in again.) But who's to say my story can't impact or inspire? Who's to say someone reading these very words aren't nodding in agreement and saying, "Yes, sis! Me, too!" That's the point.

When we share our stories and our journeys, we give a gentle hand squeeze to ladies who need confirmation that they're not alone. When we share our purpose, we give love and light to women who need that extra push to keep moving. We are all responsible for each other. Empowered women empower women, and we are essential to the "lean in" factor.

So how does that all relate to me?

What does purpose mean to me now (I'm sure you're asking)?

Let's think of it this way. I still have absolutely no clue where I'm headed, but I'm content in knowing where I am right now is exactly where I'm supposed to be. For me, purpose involves waking up every morning, choosing gratitude, counting all my blessings, and learning how to be content with not knowing what to do next.

Purpose is not a destination. There's no one thing you have to do to reach it or experience it or share it. Purpose is a journey, a never-ending story that's different from everyone else's. Purpose is about learning you, discovering your passion and being open to choosing progress over complacency every minute of every day. It's about being unafraid to fail, and understanding failures are what got you this far in the first place. It's about showing gratitude for all the choices you've made — great and tragic — and being unapologetic about them. It's about inspiring others.

We all have a story — a purpose — and it's our responsibility to share it.

So, I ask again: By a show of hands, who knows what their purpose is?

If your hand is still on the table like mine, know that it's okay to be a little clueless. Believe it or not, most of us still are.

About Kiara Anthony

Kiara Anthony is an established content developer, communicator and creative. She is a proud graduate of Towson University, earning a Bachelor of Arts degree in Mass Communication in 2013. She then pursued her master's degree in Communications at Trinity Washington University, graduating in 2015.

Within her professional career, Kiara has written and edited for entertainment blogs, nonprofit websites and online magazines, all following search engine optimization (SEO) best practices. Her communications background blends well with her knack for technical writing, ensuring client content communicates effectively and expertly to various audiences. She currently serves as a Communications Specialist within the healthtech industry.

Personally, Kiara is an active member of Zeta Phi Beta Sorority, Incorporated, devoted to the principles of Scholarship, Service, Sisterhood and Finer Womanhood. She continues to follow her commitment to community service within her dedication to The LadyBUGS, a 501c(3) mentoring organization committed to ensuring every girl is empowered and works to empower others. Most recently she joined The Loveliness Network, LLC (TLN), a dedicated platform focused on elevating the voices of Black women through storytelling. As TLN's Chief Communication Officer, Kiara helps bring the brand to life through creative content, communication strategy and a dash of personality.

Finding Your Light in Darkness

A'Dia Gaskins

In the dark, you tend to find the light when you least expect it. I've always been infatuated with learning about other cultures. Since I was a child, experiencing various foods, traditions and languages captured my attention. My first experience abroad to Jamaica, at age nine, broadened my perspective in better understanding others. Traveling provided me with two life lessons. The first is that it is important to respect other groups of people, despite your differences. The second and most critical lesson of the two, is that the world is much bigger than you. The world doesn't owe you anything.

I did not understand the true meaning of these lessons until my late teenage years. As a child, there was always that nagging desire to prove my worthiness to others. Whether that was being a "model student" or reading so much that I recited random facts verbatim, I just wanted to prove that I was worth being around. The insecurity of being alone was a harsh reality. The longing to solidify my worth was a toxic mindset, and it was extremely stressful. I had to learn that I didn't owe the world anything.

As a young child, I experienced so much stress that it became a sense of normalcy. I had plenty of it in recent years matriculating through undergraduate and graduate school with a schedule so jam packed that I had to fit in mealtimes. This was good stress. You know, the one that comes with excitement. Whether it is a new job, planning a wedding, or booking a vacation, that kind of stress can be prioritized and broken down until it becomes a simple to-do list. It's manageable. But there is also the unwavering, unmoving stress. The stuff that even your spirit can't shake. That soul-consuming, negative vibe inducing stress. It affects all of us differently. However, I found a trend with this stress. It tends to come in the most inopportune moment.

It was the year that I thought nothing could go wrong. I had obtained my master's degree and secured a job that I actually enjoyed.

My high stress indicators, tension in my back, a fluctuating appetite, and headaches were ongoing. I tried to breathe through them and manage the negative thoughts that clouded my head. I felt stagnant and unsuccessful. Even with a graduate degree, I felt unsuccessful! Fighting my thoughts, I quickly tried to determine what made me genuinely happy. Although I enjoyed my job, it wasn't something I was passionate about. I didn't live and breathe for it.

What was my purpose?

I couldn't answer a simple question. My mind was blocked with thoughts of self-doubt and apprehension.

Other external factors didn't help the situation either. Issues with relationships, not to mention family health scares, had occurred throughout the year. Quickly, it all became too much. "It's only up from here" was my mantra as I traveled halfway across the world for reprieve. I was grateful for this break in routine. My experience in Egypt was positively life- altering.

Surprisingly, Egypt was the first of its kind. It was a chance to take a spiritual journey. I needed to erase the doubt, apprehension and fear I was experiencing. I hadn't meditated in years. On this trip, I meditated twice a day. I also took to writing down my thoughts, things I learned, things I saw, and what I was grateful for. It was sudden. All it took was me looking at a picture of myself on a camel in front of the Pyramids of Giza. As I reflected on the many ancient sites before me, that I often dreamed of and read about as a child, I had an abrupt realization. By focusing on myself, clearing my mind and body of negative energy, and experiencing joy for the first time in months, I was able to define my purpose.

My purpose is *education.*

I don't mean education in its traditional form. I want to educate people on the various cultures of the world through creative writing. I want to influence people to experience culture through travel. This should have been a no-brainer due to my love for travel and literature.

The highlights of my adventures are increasing others' desire to travel by narrating my experiences. The idea would have come to me quicker had I not allowed my thoughts to be consumed by negativity, allowing stress to cloud my judgement. After that year, I had determined that I needed to figure out ways to best manage bad stress.

I have a six-step approach to maintaining my stress level. It's all about your **E.N.E.R.G.Y.**

Continue Enduring

Perseverance. Bad stress can be difficult to deal with. It can affect your health, your relationships, and even your ability to function daily. The first and most critical step to maintaining your stress level is understanding why you are stressed and proving to yourself that you are stronger than these obstacles by enduring. I found that writing helped with organizing my jumbled thoughts, throwing all negative thoughts on paper. Using the journal quickly became routine; it was a way to cleanse my thoughts so I could have receptive energy. Putting positive energy, thoughts and feelings out into the universe is essential to maintaining stress.

Sustain Nutrition

We hate to hear it, but, "You are what you eat." The food you place into your body is used to support your body's ability to operate. Healthy nutrition should be a tool that assures your body has foods that promote a better mood, energy levels and physical health. Now, I like junk food and sweets as much as anyone; however, I have found that moderation and substitutes, as annoying as they are, can be extremely helpful. It's amazing how you feel with small life changes. Wise words from one of my mentors was helpful when thinking of nutrition: "Garbage in, garbage out."

Positive Exchanges

Who you associate yourself with is important. Interactions with other humans, whether family, friends or those of the romantic kind, are critical for human development. How we interact with others, and vice versa, can impact our thoughts and energy. You want to ensure that your interactions are positive. Although we can't control the actions and words of others, we can control our reaction when dealing with difficult individuals and situations. Unfortunately, sometimes you may have to separate yourself from others when situations become upsetting. Specifically, I'm speaking on exchanges that conflict with our personal values and those exchanges that cause self-doubt and anxiety. Those types of exchanges can affect your ability to maintain positive energy. You may need to reflect on the conversation and how it made you feel before proceeding to address others about how it affected you and why. I'm a firm believer of living by the Golden Rule: "Treat others as you wish to be treated."

Restore Yourself

Walking. Meditation. Painting. It is important to find healthy techniques to help with redirecting negative energy into positive energy. Restoring yourself ensures that you do not feed negativity. Meditation was my technique in dealing with and managing my overloaded level of bad stress. While meditating, I often found myself arguing with myself about the reasons for my stress, fear and doubt. Even now, I use meditation as a coping mechanism to deal with the self-doubt and self-induced fear. It's important to have your preferred technique to bring you back to yourself. It also helps to have your go-to mantras. Mine are simple and quite popular: Faith over fear and the energy you place into the universe is what you will receive.

Be Grateful

Be appreciative. Find gratitude in the smallest things. You may have stubbed your toe getting out of bed. The kids may be yelling, and you can hear them down the hall. However, that deserves a smile because you can feel and hear. It's important to be thankful. No matter how bad my days get, I try to find at least one thing to smile about. It can be raining cats and dogs outside, without an end in sight. I still try to change my outlook on the situation. The rain may cancel a few plans, but the Earth is being cleansed. When negative thoughts roam around your head, finding something to be grateful for can be tough. But if you can find just one small thing to appreciate, I'm sure the list will continue to grow.

Remain Youthful

Although my body may age, my heart and spirit will remain young and free. Find comfort in things that bring you joy, whether that's being with nature, learning the latest dance trends, or even watching your favorite movies. Do it! Your heart and mind will thank you!

Bad stress is going to come your way. Managing stress properly will keep you from shutting down. If you find positive techniques to manage stress, and focus on influences that positively impact your energy, that small light gradually builds in the dark. Make sure you watch your energy. Make sure that no one, not even yourself, disrupts your path. Remember, the world doesn't owe you anything, and you don't owe anything back to her.

About A'Dia Gaskins

A'Dia Gaskins received her bachelor's degree from North Carolina Agricultural & Technical State University and a Master of Business Administration from Trinity Washington University. During the day, the DC native enjoys her work in Compensation and Performance Management. Other times, she is immersed in a good book, experiencing new cuisine, or planning her next adventure. Traveling as a little girl provided an early start to her passion- learning about other cultures. A perfect day for A'Dia is waking up in a different city or country or time at the beach. She currently resides in the city that she loves most.

Cycical

Amber C. Slade

I have found that my personal journey toward purpose is recurrent. Life moves so swiftly that we are in a new season before we can realize it.

Each step of my life has come with a test that led to something bigger. Every time I feel like I've figured the constant "it" out, a game changer is sure to follow. For better or worse, each of those occurrences have helped me in the long-run--when they were beautiful and even when they hurt.

I have experienced some really trying times, including verbal abuse, unfulfilling relationships, grief, job loss, and some truly debilitating anxiety. I must also acknowledge that I have experienced God's grace and mercy, as well: two healthy pregnancies and children, completion of higher education, a fulfilling and loving relationship, amazing friends, a stable home, strong health, a supportive extended family, and the list goes on.

In the spring of 2013, I was in a season of "no". Every job and graduate program I pursued told me, "No". I was a senior at North Carolina A&T State University with a proud 3.24 GPA. A political science major with all of these grand plans—but none of them were working out. After months of applications to school counseling graduate programs, five schools declined me. Every back-up part-time and full-time job I interviewed for turned me down, as well. In eight months' time, I submitted forty-seven applications and attended twenty interviews. Many of those interviews went into the final rounds. As many times as I saw hope, the rejection emails kept rolling in. At that point, I just knew I was meant to be a school counselor. I met every minimum requirement for the programs. Education was an area I was meant to be associated with, and counseling was something I was always interested in. It was the perfect combination of my interests and skills.

I always considered myself prepared and a strong interviewer. So, what was going on? I found myself, five months after graduating from college, a cashier at a popular hardware store. I was confused and even embarrassed. I have to acknowledge that there is absolutely nothing wrong with working as a cashier, no matter your level of education. It just wasn't in my plan. Little did I know, I was exactly where I was supposed to be.

While working as a cashier, I met all types of people who shared their personal stories with me. I enjoyed learning more about their personal experiences and understanding how they navigate life. I've always been fascinated by what motivates people to make the decisions they make. My experience with that specific set of people confirmed that I wanted to always be involved in something that allowed me to learn about other people and their stories.

While working there, I also ended up finding a program at North Carolina Central University called "Career Counseling & Placement". A family member, who is a licensed school counselor, told me about it. I took a little time to review it and attended a virtual info session. The next thing I knew, I was applying without really understanding what the focus was. I believe that chapter of my life humbled me to be open to opportunities that come when you aren't looking for them. It was my reminder that God guides my steps and protects me, even when I'm not asking Him to.

After a few interview rounds, I was accepted. In that moment, I felt like I could breathe again just from seeing the "congratulations" at the top of that email. I felt as though I had direction. I had absolutely no idea where it would take me, but it felt good to take on a new challenge. My parents were elated. My Dad even said, "I knew you could do it. Now, what can you do with that?" My response was, "I'm not exactly sure, but I think I can go into training or HR. I know it's something that lets me work with people in education settings. I'll figure it out."

He said, "I know you will."

One week later, to the day, he had a massive stroke. I was halted. I was nervous for my mom, but optimistic that he would recover. A little under two weeks until my birthday is when I got the call from my mom.

"Your faith is strong. He's gone, baby. He's gone." The last time I spoke with him (the day of the stroke), his words sounded so final. I was asking him a thousand questions over the phone about financial aid and buying cars. He said, "I trust you to figure it out. I want your life to be perfect. I trust your judgment." Little did I know, that was the last time I'd speak to him. He stayed in the hospital for about seven weeks and died from complications on January 14, 2015, my ninth day of graduate school.

Panic and devastation overcame me. I questioned God's decision and timing. I was so angry that He was making me live the rest of my life without my dad. He was my go-to person, my protector, and life advisor. He was gone and he wasn't coming back.

The next day, I reached out to my advisor and expressed that I would need to leave the program. It was the only thing that made sense at the time. I just knew my life was going to be drastically different than how I'd imagined it. She and another instructor offered nothing but grace and support. Their seamless approach to that situation helped me get where I am today.

I ended up staying in the program and taking off for about two weeks while staying home in Pennsylvania. I came back around to the coursework, and it was exactly what I needed. Career Counseling and Placement is an extension of traditional mental health counseling with an added component of career development theories and practices. At our core, we are trained as mental health professionals. Through my coursework and readings, I was steeped in counseling techniques and healthier ways of navigating difficult situations. I applied it all to my personal life. Educationally, I was in a great spot. Emotionally, I was fragile. I couldn't make it through a discussion board or even a car ride without weeping.

Three months after my dad passed, I found out I was pregnant with my first child. During an ultrasound, the tech paused and said,

"Actually, your due date won't be December 24. It's going to get pushed a little...to January 3." My dad's birthday is January 3. A few moments later she asked, "Would you like to know the sex?"

I nodded affirmatively.

"It's a boy," she said calmly. I cried immediately.

As I've mentioned, I'm a believer of God and eternal life. I know my dad is in Paradise and has not been reincarnated to this world. But there is no doubt in my mind that he influenced my child's soul before he got here. What broke my heart the most is that my dad was such a family and community-oriented person. I always saw him interacting with other kids and coaching. Yet, my children would never get to know him. Well, on January 2, 2016, Blake Matthew entered the world. He showed up thirteen days into a new semester! I was beyond tired, but I finished that semester with two A's and graduated the following May in 2017.

How does this tie into my purpose? I spend my days helping students and individuals navigate their academic, personal and career goals. I help them prepare for interviews, job searches, internships, graduate/law/medical school, choosing their majors, and more. These are the same areas I failed miserably at just a few years ago. Through a simple resume review, I help people confidently speak about themselves. Just as my advisors provided grace and a smooth transition during my time of grief, I get to offer that same sense of support to the people I work with. I try to help people navigate where their story is headed while encouraging them to keep an open mind to what life (God) brings to them.

After some time in my new role, I met my fiancé. He is the person who encourages me to be my authentic self and loves Blake as his own. He was also not in the original plan, but he is exactly the person I needed. Those obstacles led me to motherhood, my partner, and my calling: to continually heal myself and others; to leave people better than I found them; to showcase God's power through my own life.

While I have a career, area of expertise, fancy letters behind my name, and a shiny title in higher education right now, this is not my last stop. I believe a person's purpose changes throughout their life. Mine will, too, again and again. I see it on the horizon very soon.

About Amber C. Slade

My name is Amber Slade and I currently reside in Greensboro, NC with my fiance and two beautiful boys, Blake Matthew and Tristan Brian. I am truly in awe and most grateful that God gave me the unique assignment to be their Mother. I grew up in Harrisburg, PA and enjoy spending time with my extended family each opportunity I have to travel home.

I hold a Bachelor's degree in Political Science from North Carolina A&T State University and Master's degree in Career Counseling from North Carolina Central University. As a Career Advisor at a local liberal arts College, I spend my time helping students explore and prepare for their goals and interests in the classroom and beyond.

Ultimately, I believe in more than producing professional robots, but helping people become more self-aware individuals who hold the confidence to write and rewrite their own stories time and time again.

Finding My Wings: A Story of Unearthing My Authentic Self

Ashley Peterson

"We delight in the beauty of the butterfly, but rarely admit the changes it has gone through to achieve that beauty."

– Maya Angelou

At the start of 2018, I found myself sitting in a feeling I hadn't felt before. At home, I struggled to rest and sleep peacefully, yet, I felt uncomfortable if I was not one with my bed and bundle of pillows. At work, I was accomplishing tasks, but feeling like I wasn't making any true impact and like I didn't belong. With family and friends, I slowly disconnected because I was losing who I was and couldn't bear them to know or to worry about me. I was a lost soul in a fully functioning body, experiencing depression for the first time, but fearful of asking for help.

But this is not about the depression. It's about how I unlocked the power within myself through self-reflection driven by therapy. It's about what I learned to overcome it, while finding and accepting my authentic self in the process.

Prior to this time, I had a vivid dream about why God put me on this earth - my purpose. I was placed here to be a light for others, to share my journey *and* imperfections, and to inspire those looking up to me at all ages. I saw it, I understood it, I knew how I was living in it so far in small ways, but I didn't understand how powerful it could be if I walked in it fully. My roller coaster of experiences in life and my quiet, modest nature kept me from having the confidence to show that my successes were balanced with a share of mishaps and mistakes. So, in this time of losing myself, I made myself believe that maybe I interpreted this purpose incorrectly. There was no way that the woman who was going through life seen as an inspiration to others was literally crumbling.

In the spring of 2018, I hit rock bottom. Not asking for help was no longer an option. I had therapy in the back of my mind for a while, but I hadn't done research to understand what I truly needed. I made the initial decision to seek help through a local cognitive behavioral therapist and, because finding a therapist is like finding a true friend or partner, I unfortunately experienced red flags that resulted in an unsuccessful pairing.

While I was slightly disheartened, I did not let this deter me. I leaned in to my still burning desire to finally ask for the support I desperately needed. I quickly turned to the app, Talkspace, where I was thankfully matched with a therapist who has truly become a lifeline because of, what I know now to be, our shared understanding of life as young professional Black women. As I shared my experiences and what I was going through, she immediately understood the why. She understood exactly what got me to this breaking point. I was ready to allow my authentic self to show in a space without judgement. I was now willingly removing the superwoman cape without looking back.

Over the past three years, that instant connection not only helped me overcome the troubling experiences that brought me to her, but we've unpacked deep-rooted habits and insecurities that have silenced my true self. After three years, I have found the authentic Ashley who has been waiting to bloom and embrace her wings for the world to see. I was ready to walk in that purpose and be more open to showing how I almost got off track.

In line with being a light to those who may need similar guidance or inspiration, here are five things I have learned in my journey to becoming my authentic self:

#1 Absolutely No One Is Perfect

Yes, we may hear this a lot, but the repetition is 110% necessary. One of the hardest things to overcome was thinking I had to keep up the public perception that my life was "perfect" when I was drowning behind my smile and optimism. Was it okay for someone who seemingly had it all together to suddenly say she was struggling with depression? The answer was absolutely - not only for my own sanity, but to show others that you can still achieve amazing things despite obstacles.

#2 Mental Wellness is a Lifelong Journey, Starting With YOU

It was my decision to choose therapy, but the decision before that was to choose me above all. Whatever path you choose to support your holistic well-being, be patient and give yourself grace as you figure out what works for you. The decisions and work you do now will set you up to be more prepared and flexible to support the twists and turns, and unexpected events, of life. As you approach new chapters in life, today's approach may need to change, but the foundation of self is the most important part of getting through. Remember, you cannot be there for anyone else—personally or professionally—without being there for yourself first.

#3 Growth Is Uncomfortable, At Any Age

In that path of putting myself first, I had to accept a lot of uncomfortable things within me, while approaching the milestone of thirty. I had to accept why friendships and relationships were not going as smoothly as I wanted them to. I had to accept why I was passionate about my work, but I couldn't speak up for myself when needed. I had to accept why I was carrying burdens that were not mine. When my therapist began our work to uncover things that I didn't want to believe impacted me, I actually "hid" from her for multiple months out of fear of acknowledgement and needing to adopt change. In my journey to authenticity and transparency, I made mistakes, but the most important part was that I forgave myself first and accepted that I would not grow from constant comfort and success only.

#4 Your Authentic Self Will Remove People & Things You'd Never Dream of Losing

If I look back over the past few years, my life is simply different. Once that flip of the switch came, and I embraced my authentic self, I physically, mentally and emotionally felt the evolution. I became more comfortable with not coming off as a perfect human being. I maintained reasonable expectations. I leaned into my truth, and I found myself getting less disappointed by the actions of others. I was finally seeing the world for what it was, and the people in it for who they chose to be, not who I hoped they would be. When I found my wings to guide me to and through my purpose, I realized I still needed a support system to keep me going. That support system quickly became the ones who needed to be there instead of those that I wanted there.

#5 Depression Does Not Just Go Away; You Learn to Manage It

If you are like me, and you may be navigating the impacts of depression, remember that the true success is learning how to manage it. As we navigated the pandemic, well after I thought I was "healed", I found myself experiencing my second depressive episode. I thought I was navigating 2020 well, but a series of back-to-back events at the beginning of 2021 showed me that I was not. I was slowly slipping backward. That growth I was experiencing put me in a place of not just processing what was happening in the world around us, but also trying to understand this new Ashley that was forming her wings. It was layers upon layers of change and adjustment, but I was thankful to have the tools to recognize it and managed to save myself from falling too far off track once again.

For my 28th birthday, I gifted myself with a tattoo of a unalome symbol on my right forearm, strategically placed for me to see all day long. The unalome symbol represents the path to enlightenment in the Buddhist culture, symbolizing the twists and turns in life that lead to peace and harmony before we reach the closing chapter in our lives.

This is not just a reminder of my journey that, at the time, was still in its infancy stages, but of that purpose that I almost allowed myself to deny. Instead, I now understand that being perfectly imperfect is fine. Each day is going to represent a new start to understand my full self and to share that with others. Three years after that moment of experiencing rock bottom, I am not just embracing my purpose, but I wake up every morning with the full intent of being who I am, unapologetically.

By sharing this story, I am giving my butterfly a voice, encouraging you to pause, embrace your journey, and seek the power within yourself. We are all born with a butterfly within us, but it is our choice to allow it to gain its wings and flourish.

About Ashley Peterson

Ashley Peterson is a Human Resources professional in the financial services industry, skilled in the areas of employee communications, career development, and Diversity, Equity, Inclusion & Belonging. Driven by her passions for mentorship and mental health awareness, she takes pride in being a storyteller, providing insight into her own personal and professional experiences to help others. Over the past decade, Ashley has been proud to lead and serve in programs focused on the total wellness and development of high school and college students, and fellow corporate professionals. Ashley completed her Bachelor's in Marketing at North Carolina Agricultural & Technical State University, Master's in Integrated Marketing Communications at West Virginia University, and is a member of Delta Sigma Theta Sorority, Inc. Born and raised in New Jersey, Ashley has been able to experience living in various regions throughout her career and currently resides in Charlotte, NC.

Lifting Our Voices and My Own

Dr. Khalyn Solomon

"Be bold enough to use your voice, brave enough to listen to your heart, and strong enough to live the life you've always imagined."

—*Unknown*

For as long as I can remember, my grandfather represented a hodgepodge of attributes. He was one of a kind. A man who had lived a beautifully complicated life at such an early age — a story all too common for many of our Black men.

Papa's not with us anymore, but man, oh man, do I cherish my memories with him. His big bear hugs, especially when he'd pick us up after school. His jokes, even when he wasn't trying to make them (which only made us laugh even harder). And of course, his one-of-a-kind voice, a voice that commanded respect, but was also filled with a sense of warmth, compassion and wisdom. Only recently have I started to realize that Papa was one of the first people who instilled in me how powerful the voice can truly be – as it holds the potential to lift others, while also lifting yourself.

You ever think you have a plan and that you have it all figured out? If you're not there yet, trust me, you will be. It was the fall of 2009 and my senior year in high school. If you asked me then, I already knew what my plans would be after graduation. I would attend Howard University, study Print Journalism, and start my own magazine. I guess you could say I was channeling my inner Khadijah James (cues "Living Single" theme song).

I absolutely loved to write. I was an editor for my high school's newspaper and my teachers encouraged me to continue down that path after graduation. Imagine my surprise when my mom had another plan in mind. Seriously? This was my first "adult" decision. I was almost eighteen and totally knew what was best for me. I giggle when I think back to that moment. I was still a kid, but you couldn't tell me a thing. Grown and all, however, my mom still changed my plans.

She'd determined that majoring in Speech-Language Pathology would be a better fit for me. I'd never in my life heard of that major and I could not believe she didn't support my journalistic dreams. She's a healthcare provider and thought I would be able to do the same, while integrating my passion of writing, speaking and helping others.

Fast forward to that next summer. Things changed and I didn't go to Howard. Instead, I moved to Greensboro, North Carolina on a full scholarship to attend another HBCU: North Carolina A&T. Although it wasn't a part of my plan, I was beyond excited and grateful. Many members of my family had attended A&T, including Papa. At the time, he was still living and was filled with so much pride that I, too, would be attending his beloved alma mater.

I loved A&T! I played in the marching band. I really enjoyed campus life, and I had already made some friends. When it was the first day of class, however, I internally kicked and screamed as I walked past a journalism class and entered "Intro to Speech-Language Pathology" instead. I sat down at a desk and blankly stared at the white board before our professor entered the room. Fifty minutes later, I was completely convinced that this major was a good fit for me. Imagine my mom's delight (and sarcasm) as I called and told her I'd had a slight change of heart.

I get this question a lot: "What exactly is Speech-Language Pathology?" It's a profession that focuses on the treatment of people of all ages who present with various communication disorders. From a toddler who's a late talker to an adult who's rebuilding their ability to speak after a stroke, Speech-Language Pathologists provide much more than therapy. They realize that every person deserves a voice, and they help them get there.

To practice in the Speech profession, you have to have a master's degree. So, four years later, I moved to Tallahassee, Florida to attend Florida State University (FSU) for graduate school. I remember my first day of orientation for the program like it was yesterday. I walked into the Speech Clinic and quickly realized that there was nobody else who looked like me in my class. I was the only Black student. What a stark contrast from A&T where everybody looked just like me. This made sense though because the majority of Speech Pathologists in our country are White women. In fact, 8% of Speech Pathologists identify as a racial minority. I still haven't been able to find what percentage identify as Black.

During my first semester at FSU, my grandfather passed away. His health had been up and down that year. I remember going to visit him at the hospital back home and, ironically, he had been receiving speech therapy. Although a graduate student, I still wanted to learn from his Speech Pathologist in order to help him outside of therapy. Just as he had lifted my voice as a little girl, I was now, in a way, lifting his.

Overall, I had a great experience at FSU. I participated in hands-on clinical rotations and conducted lots of research. However, I also quickly learned that I had to work twice as hard to earn my degree. From fellow classmates questioning my worthiness of being accepted into the program, to some patients outwardly indicating their biases as it pertained to Black people, I knew I had to always, always, always be on point and do my best. Was it fair? No way. But, as we all were reminded this past year, unfairness and inequality seems all too familiar for African Americans in this country.

Nonetheless, I think my experiences at FSU pushed me to become more interested in the Doctorate in Speech-Language Pathology (SLPD) program. I had learned more about the degree while attending a national Speech Pathology conference as a graduate student. When I showed interest, however, I was told by a Black Speech Pathologist who had received their SLPD that I probably wouldn't be admitted until I had more experience under my belt—at least five to seven years of experience. To be honest, I felt a little discouraged at that moment. I expected to be motivated and uplifted by someone who looked like me, but I wasn't. After two years of working as a Speech Pathologist, however, I decided to apply to various Doctorate in Speech-Language

Pathology programs. Although the Speech Pathologist at the conference told me I wouldn't get in, I decided to listen to my voice instead.

What do you know? I was accepted! I was able to earn my Doctorate in Speech-Language Pathology from Northwestern University. Imagine my surprise when I walked into orientation and saw five other Black students this time around. This immediately told me that Black Speech-Language Pathologists' much needed presence within this profession was growing! The six of us supported each other constantly and continue to remain great friends to this day.

My experience at Northwestern was fulfilling and it challenged me in ways I hadn't imagined, both academically and personally. Graduation was scheduled for March 20, 2020, a week after COVID-19 was officially declared a global pandemic. Although I wasn't able to fully celebrate, I was inspired and motivated by Northwestern's SLPD program to continue to lift my voice by lifting the voices of children of color, too. In this moment, I decided to establish my pediatric private practice, The Speech Exchange.

At The Speech Exchange, our mission is to enhance the lives of all children with communication disorders by providing transformative speech therapy, offering support for their families, and ensuring that the entire journey toward healing is accessible, comforting and successful. We also focus on providing services to children of color, as well as children living in underserved communities.

What I've realized on my journey thus far is that helping others actually helps me, too. It grants me a sense of purpose … a sense of self. Simply put, it makes me happy. I'm still learning and I'm still growing. But what I'd like to share with you is a personal guide that helps me lift my voice as I continue to develop a deeper understanding of myself – all while I aim to lift the voices of others, too. I hope it guides you as much as it guides me.

8 Tools to Help Lift Your Voice

1. Have faith in yourself.
2. Set healthy boundaries with others.

3. Meet yourself with compassion.
4. Be flexible.
5. Don't compare your journey to others' journeys.
6. Trust that you made the right decision.
7. Surround yourself with good people.
8. Keep smiling.

I think back to my eighteen-year-old self, giving Papa the biggest hug before leaving for college. All my life, he lifted me up with his direction, his wisdom, his voice. Ten years later, I now aspire to do the same.

About Dr. Khalyn Solomon

Dr. Khalyn Solomon is a pediatric speech-language pathologist and owner of The Speech Exchange and Language Therapy, Inc. She received her B.A. in Speech-Language Pathology from North Carolina A&T State University, her M.S. in Speech-Language Pathology from Florida State University, and her Doctorate in Speech-Language Pathology from Northwestern University.

Khalyn has received numerous awards during her graduate studies including "Most Outstanding First Year Clinician" and the "College Leadership Award". At Northwestern, Khalyn's culminating research focused on "Guiding Speech-Language Assessment Principles for Underserved Pediatric Populations". The project offered an in-depth look into what current speech-language diagnostic practices may be affecting intervention qualifications for underserved pediatric communities. She is passionate about advocating for the equal rights of all children within the speech-language profession.

Originally from Atlanta, Georgia, this is Khalyn's fourth year living in Southern California. She enjoys traveling, trying different restaurants, and exploring new and exciting places in the Golden State.

Self-Determination: Transforming My Pain Into Power

Ipeleng Motuba

There lies great diversity between doing it all and having it all. The former requires persistence, resilience and self-determination. The latter requires knowing how to explore boundaries. Some people attend to their purpose as they do existence, without knowing that one ought to delve beyond such existence to achieve that purpose. As a child, people always referred to me as having great "potential". This compliment was not received because I was ashamed for existing as a person with unfulfilled potential. I seldom envisioned my life beyond high school. I only held certainty toward becoming a professional sportswoman. Our mother simultaneously developed a motive for me to move to New York. It now suffices that these juxtaposed dreams could not co-exist. From a spiritual perspective, they were never intended. As the youngest of four girls, I was spoiled with a traditional home filled with food, true love in the air, and the fierce protection that only comes about having older sisters. We were raised with freedom and full support of our individuality. We understand the essence of community. Where we come from, community equates to muscle. Our family is a force of nature and humility alike. In discovering myself within this nuclear structure, most people found me to be lost. But I always had an inkling for the journey ahead. I knew then that the pain of experiencing loss would constantly follow me and that I would have to will survival by constantly turning it into a superpower.

December 26, 2007 was a family Christmas by the beach. In a few days, I would be turning eighteen. Due to my being a lazy scholar, low grades compelled me to drop out of my dream sports tournament. If I had been a better academic scholar, I would have accomplished the ultimate goal of becoming a member of the South African Women's Hockey Team. For thirteen years, this failure has haunted me. But I have had to move past that dream. Now and then, when I see a gold medal on television, my heart feels sore. Some days, it is in response to that dream. Others, it is because I know that the gold used to meld those prizes was stolen from my country and the world does not care. From the age of four, I aspired to fulfill the shoes of Venus and Serena Williams, Arantxa Sanchez Vicario and Marion Jones. The novel uncertainty of my future did not deter me, but I could not have been prepared for the calamity that ensued.

My sisters and I were lounging around the house after the previous day's Christmas extravaganza. As the mid-morning sun ascended, and swarms of domestic workers were set free to spread their joy across the shore, our mom decided to go for a run. She ran daily. We were accustomed to her love for adventure. But, on this particular day, the sun was burning hot and the streets festive. As an independent doer, she ignored our pleas and we bid her adieu. The heartache that followed was unimaginable. Our mother never returned from that fateful run. After many hours of searching for her, while always remaining calm, her spirit filled my soul and whispered that we are always going to be together.

It was later discovered that she had drowned in the ocean. Thirteen years later, the pain has yet to subside. The days that followed are one. We held the funeral before the year's end, and we inevitably survived. Survival is the primary purpose I have had since that day. I gained minor independence by attempting to use my measly grades to attend law school. I developed a newfound respect for the traditions of our household and instantaneously absorbed her ability to network.

My tertiary academic journey dwindled significantly, and this was strenuous for everyone around me. After many years of failure, I decided to stop being an outlaw. With the grace of our father, I enrolled in culinary school. I had been working as a chef while trying to pursue my undergraduate law degree. Again, I found myself under the majesty of juxtaposed ambitions. I built a professional reputation that allowed me to work in many restaurants, sharing in others' pain along the way. I spent every penny in my pocket, traveling the world. At some point, I measured all expenditure in relation to purchasing a plane ticket. After the passing of our mother, I tried my best to adapt to societal norms, but I could not. I felt suffocated and pushed all the boundaries that one could conceive. Our selfless father encouraged me throughout this difficult time, and we grew together in our new life. Our mother raised us as children, and he is raising us as adults.

I went on to enjoy an exciting culinary career, even running my own catering company. I was especially proud that I had overcome the hurdle of formal education. We do not have the same perception of shared experiences. But I know that, through the rebellion and experimentation, I was not the greatest example of a model child. This is how I came to understand forgiveness. For every shame that I have been forgiven, there rests an inner-child paving the way for her thirty-something-year-old self to spread her magic, as she should have. As she always could. As they always knew she would.

In 2015, I moved out of my hometown to work as a chef. I worked myself to the bone and experienced a loneliness that I have yet to interpret. It soon dawned on me that the fantasy was meant to remain such. I found myself truly mourning our mother for the first time. I could not reach out to her to seek counsel. I had spent the past eight years gallivanting around the world, broke and surviving through human interaction. I had not accomplished my dream. It had failed once more. The end of that year resulted in my losing two jobs, being evicted from my apartment, and moving back home shy of a degree. I recall sitting at my desk in Johannesburg, staring through my soul and deciding that I should return to law school. They were right: It is important to have something to fall back on. As dark of a lesson as this was, I was better prepared to attack school again. I had the benefit of work experience, travel, a network, and the art of human interaction. In hindsight, had our mother continued to live, I most likely would have remained unconscious to the experience of love beyond reasonable doubt and self-correction beyond measure. The precipitating intimate qualities, solely catalyzed by trauma of the soul.

Today, most people look at me, perplexed as to how, when, or why. I can see in their eyes. I urge them not to ponder for only I know what it has taken to sacrifice my being, to combust into this world. What it takes to be revered dynamic. The scenic route has been grueling, but

I am here. I carry the pain in my heart, reminded of the order of my world. On most days, I am compounded by memory and loss. I chose to move close to the ocean because I find solace in our mother being there.

I always wish I had accompanied her. What kind of sportswoman leaves her mother to go running alone? *These were formerly insignificant thoughts that often passed through me.* Then, I remind myself that I am not a sportswoman. I think about the way she would bathe me when I was sick. The fierce support she showed me on the sidelines of the field. Her kiss.

In our culture, there is a Setswana maxim that loosely translates to, "A person is made humane through experiencing the humanity of others." I am made so by way of our patient, devoted, and most gregarious father. We have created this opportunity to further my education in the United States because we are deserving. I am here to teach, as I have been taught by those who fought through oppression to ensure this privilege.

One of my greatest teachers was my paternal grandmother. She, too, sacrificed her life for me to expel my deepest fear of not reaching that potential. As she once exclaimed to us (at a time when we were too young to understand and in too much trouble to ask), "He who laughs last laughs the best!" I owe it to myself to continue to inspire, love and believe. Self-determination is my only substance of choice. Every day, I choose the power because it lies within me. This renewed journey was written before my time. I am healing. I am doing it all. I have it all. Those who have gone before me live within those who walk beside me. Today is my solemn comfort. Tomorrow, a mystery.

About Ipeleng Motuba

My name is Ipeleng Motuba. I am a South African woman, chef and graduate student enrolled at the University of Southern California (USC) Gould School of Law. I am passionate about refugee law, immigration, penal reform, women and children's rights. I have worked primarily with Black migrant families from across the Africancontinent whose stories remain unrecognized. I am deeply disturbed by the invisible status society seems to perpetually impose on Black communities. My life experience has pushed me to think creatively about the role of film narrative in shaping public policy, public opinion and most of all, providing opportunities for others to be visible, seen and heard; hence my undertaking a specialization in entertainment law. I aspire to cultivate my legal experience in the United States and bring that back to South Africa to address law and policy that enhances sports and career opportunities for girls and disadvantaged youth

Finding Fit

Jameice DeCoster

I was nine years old, and it was my first track meet. I was so excited and nervous, with adrenaline running all throughout my veins. I got on the line for the 100-meter run. The gunman said, "On your mark, get set, go!" I took off but began to jog. I finished the race in last place and went back to the bleachers to sit with my dad. Although I lost, he congratulated me. Before I went to warm up for my next race, he said, "Go out there and run your fastest!"

I replied, "I'm supposed to run my fastest?"

I won the rest of my races that day.

Eight years later, I was in college, running track, acquiring achievements like Big Ten All-American and, when I transferred, ACC All-American. After graduating, I kept working out because it was engrained in me. I had been an athlete since the age of nine. So being physically fit was something I knew all too well. I continually worked out like I was still in college. I thought about personal training, but I was afraid to try it because of fear of judgement. It seemed that all the college athletes who stopped competing became personal trainers. I did not want to be a part of that statistic. Do you know that feeling you get when you know you should be doing something, but you aren't doing it for whatever reason? That thought that runs across your mind every single day, telling you that you need to be doing 'that thing' that God has for you. Every time I scrolled on Instagram and saw another personal trainer or fitness influencer doing what I knew I needed to be doing, I felt convicted.

I should have been doing that, too. I knew I was not living out my full purpose or tapping into my full potential. There was so much more to me than what I was sharing. I would talk myself out of it by saying, "Oh, the market is too saturated! There are personal trainers and fitness influencers everywhere!" I also reminded myself of that same ol' college athlete who wanted to relive their athletic days by being a personal trainer. I didn't want to be like that. Five years went by before I officially decided to get out of my head and do what I knew God had called me to do!

It all started with a post on Instagram, showing the bread aisle. In the post, it showed all the different brands of bread and said something along the lines of, "Have you ever felt the market was saturated? Walk down the bread aisle in the grocery store! The way you do it is totally different (or should be)! No one person can service the whole world, so put your spin on it!" Even after seeing that post, I was not ready to take the plunge. But I couldn't get that post and the message out of my mind. It sat with me for a few more months. Then, on October 1, 2018, I began my Instagram page (@Fitmeice) and Facebook page (FitMeice). I still was not training people, but my following began to grow. People messaged me, telling me how much I encouraged them and motivated them to be the best version of themselves.

Also, in 2018, I began my Doctorate in Clinical Psychology journey. I realized my passions for health, both physical and mental, were colliding. During this time, my motto Physically Strong, Mentally Healthy ™ was born. I started to feel like I was living out my purpose by bringing together both mental and physical health. My purpose was being fulfilled and my conviction was diminishing. On January 1, 2020, I began personal training. My training model was, and still is, 100% virtual. I wanted to make working out accessible and realistic. With living in the D.C. Metropolitan area, I understand how difficult it can be with traffic to get to and from places. I also wanted women to feel comfortable working out. What better way to do that than from the comforts of your own home? My model is designed for the women who are mothers, or may be busy, or they may have gym-timidation (intimidated by the gym). When the world shut down in March of 2020 due to the pandemic, I was already working the virtual model for about two months. I felt that God knew what He was doing when He told me to create this virtual model. I, or my clients, did not have to adjust much because we were already working the virtual model.

April 2020, I started Thursday and Saturday morning bootcamps. They were immensely popular and helped people get moving during the shutdown. It was a time we could gather for an hour and challenge our bodies and our minds. At the end of each bootcamp, during our cooldown, I gave a speech, encouraging both mental and physical health. I gave suggestions on how to stay active during the pandemic and urged people to take charge of their mental health. The pandemic was difficult emotionally for many. In October of 2020, I released my first challenge of many, the "I Can Abs" challenge. That challenge lasted for twenty-one days. It consisted of daily videos of positive affirmations; video demonstrations of every exercise; a meal guide and grocery list; information on what abs are and how they are formed; and a list of FAQs.

I am aware of the health challenges in my community. While my goal is to be able to inspire all women, I gained my desire to change the health narrative from my extended family. Black people suffer from chronic diseases at higher rates than other races. Although Black people are knowledgeable about leading a healthy lifestyle, Black women have disproportionately performed lower levels of physical activity. They have been impacted by cardiometabolic disease, such as obesity and cardiovascular disease. There is some self-report data that has shown that only 39% of Black women accomplish the national physical activity recommended guidelines set by the Department of Health and Human Services of 150 minutes per week of moderate intensity (Hubbell, et al., 2019).

When I work with my clients, my first question is, "What is your why?" Losing weight for a trip or to fit into a bathing dress is not sustainable. However, when women say they want to lose weight because they have health conditions that require them to make a change; they want to be around to see their children graduate from high school; they want to be able to be active and play with their children; or set an example for their child, those women normally stick with it long-term because they have intrinsic motivation. I have many family members who suffer from controllable chronic diseases. With education and healthy food substitutions, I know they can turn their prognosis around. I want to set an example for my extended family to better not only their physical wellness, but also their mental wellness.

It's just as important to care of your body from the neck up as it is to take care of your body from the neck down! Because of my field of study in clinical psychology, I am driven to improve my community's mental and physical wellness. Currently, my dissertation is analyzing motivational factors for Black women to engage in physical activity. With that information, I plan to help develop wellness plans to help Black women get more active and take charge of their health.

Increasing wellness for all types of women is my drive but increasing wellness for Black women is my why.

About Jameice DeCoster

Jameice DeCoster (@FitMeice) is currently pursuing a doctoral degree in Clinical Psychology and also has a Masters in public health. She is also a personal trainer and fitness enthusiast, who understands the importance of the intersection between mental and physical health.

Jameice believes that the brain and the body must work together to create the best version of you. Making sure we care for our bodies from the neck down is just as important as caring for the body from the neck up. As a former Division 1 scholarship athlete in track and field, she understands firsthand, what it takes to get and keep your body in its best shape. Her motto is Physically Strong Mentally Healthy.

Purpose and Relational Intelligence

Jelina Sheppard

Purpose is the reasoning for something being done or the reason in which something is created. Purpose is a never-ending journey. There's always more to be discovered, always more layers. I'm sure my fellow authors will discuss with you some strategies on how to discover your "why" so you can understand your role in the universal motion picture. But I want to share with you purpose as it relates to relational intelligence.

Relational intelligence is a combination of learned skills and behaviors used to navigate relationships well. The higher your relational intelligence, the better your relationships should be. Purpose, then, from the lens of relational intelligence, can be viewed as a principle or life hack, if you will. If purpose is the reason behind something being done, then everything you do in life should be done out of purpose. It should have some beneficial value attached to it if you desire to live a life of purpose.

Why is that relevant to our relationships? When you connect with anyone (intimately, business partnerships, friendships, career, etc.), it should serve a purpose. I almost said "greater" but, at the very least, there needs to be some reason you're connected to who you're connected to. Someone once said the trajectory of your life can be assessed by the five individuals you spend most of your time with. Most people accept that to be factual. If you're surrounded by goal-oriented people, you will also become goal-oriented. If you're surrounded by the wealthy, you, too, should find yourself wealthy. If you're surrounded by people who complain a lot and are unsatisfied with their lives, then, as a result, you'll become unsatisfied. You will be a complainer instead of one who improves. Biblically, the principle for purpose in relational intelligence is found in Proverbs 27:17: "Iron sharpens iron."

When assessing your relationships, ask yourself, "How?" and "Why?" When trying to apply the principle of purpose in life (understanding and walking in your why), having the answers to these questions should make it easier to navigate your many "purposes". Also, before I go further into breaking down those questions, yes, I put a "s" on purpose because, like I mentioned in the beginning, our life's purpose is layered. We were created to do many things and play different roles. There may be one thing you do well. Most people assume that their purpose is connected to that one passion or talent. While I enjoy singing, today, it may not be my "purpose". It might, for now, just be my gifting. I think one of my purposes is to educate those in mathematics, but my passion for singing has nothing to do with me teaching. So many times, we think our gifting is our ultimate why. But your gift is to be shared with others. It's a gift. It may not always lead to your current purpose. Although it very well could, don't always try to force your gifting/talent into your purpose season. You might miss out on "purpose". God may need you to encourage someone else because you have the underlying gift of "encouragement" even though you're an introvert. Purpose is objective. It cares nothing about what you're comfortable doing. Purpose is designed to serve a greater need than that of your own. Sometimes the various purposes you'll serve in life may not always be connected to the thing you're most passionate about. But your purpose will always be connected to an underlying skill or gifting you possess. Now, back to relational intelligence and its correlation to purpose.

Relational Purpose Assessment

1. How am I connected to this person?

What is the nature of my relationship? Is this connection a business partnership? Is this an intimate relationship? If so, are we committed? Is this causal? Situationship? Netflix and Chill? Is this a kindred relationship, meaning family? Spiritual? What is the basis of your connection with whomever you're connected to? Some people shy away from asking, "What are we doing?" However, it's such an important question to the one with good intentions. When you have an understanding about what it is you're doing, generally, you're able to do "it" well. Understanding can correct unmet expectations and prevent frustration. When you're clear on what you're doing, hopefully (if you're a relationally intelligent being), you will play your role well.

2. Why am I connected to this person?

It may sound selfish. But first and foremost, why should I connect myself with you? Am I connected to you because, financially, there is something for my business to gain? Intimately, do you add to my peace of mind? Do you enhance my happiness? (Keep in mind, happiness is most times based on what is happening). If this is a mentor-mentee relationship, am I learning from you or are you learning from me? Is that investment of information going to yield a return? If we are friends, do you add value to my life through reliability? Is there a level of loyalty and safety I receive from you and vice versa? Because relationships are a two-way street, there should be something you're reciprocating or exchanging in return.

We've discussed taking inventory of your current relationships and how to choose the best relationships for you moving forward. But what about if you've answered, or not been able to answer, the questions above? What happens next? If you were unable to answer the questions above, or if you didn't like the understanding you received, decide if and/or how you're going to further cultivate those relationships or end them. Buckle up. This is the hard part.

In my book, Overcoming Your Breakup: A Lover's Guide to Resilience, I help you make the decision to continue the relationship or move on. Ultimately, the principle is that every relationship should make you better. It should add value to your life. Those individuals should help you bring your vision to life. Whatever it is that you picture for your relationships, the people in those relationships should be acting out the necessary roles to bring what you envision to fruition. A deeper assessment of value requires you to be objective, meaning to treat or deal with facts, without distortion by personal feelings or prejudices. Purpose doesn't care that it's your best friend. If homie or homegirl isn't adding value or helping you level up, if they aren't at least someone you can depend on, maybe they shouldn't receive so much of your time and space in your life. Let's jump into the objective questions to help you decide if the connections you have should remain or be dissolved.

Should I Maintain the Relationship?

1. Every relationship should yield a return. *What have you received in your relationship?* What do you get from your investment? After addressing this question, follow up and answer: What do you want or expect in return from your relationships? Are they willing to give you that?

2. Next, identify the purpose they will serve in the relationship. *Are they serving their purpose?* If not, is there any evidence they're progressing toward fulfilling their purpose?

3. *Are you putting in what you expect to get out?* God's principle of "iron sharpens iron" means you also have a responsibility to be iron. Galatians 6:7, Luke 6:38, and Matthew 7:20 are good Scriptures to meditate on. Whatever you sow, you will reap. If you find that you're not getting back what you're putting in, it's time to check the soil you're sowing into. Sometimes, there is nothing wrong with how you are sowing. Instead, the problem is where you're sowing. An individual who does not value reciprocity cannot sow back into you. Consider this when investing.

4. *Is the person and the relationship worth the work?* After you have addressed all three questions, spend some time evaluating this final question. Is maintaining your relationship worth the investment? Are you benefitting in some way? Is there a greater purpose being achieved? After you've gathered all the information, decide if the connection will remain or be dissolved. At the very least, decode how you will prioritize these relationships/partnerships moving forward.

Everything you do in life should have purpose. Your time is precious. Your energy is valuable, and the vision you have for your life is worth the intentionality you're manifesting. Remember, our lives are a reflection of the top five relationships where we invest most of our time. Thus, relational intelligence is a must. Relationships of purpose are life hacks. What does your life reflect?

Find the purpose in your relationships and watch you, and those individuals attached to you, thrive. Let's live on purpose!

About Jelina Sheppard

J. Sheppard, formally known as Jelina Sheppard, is an author, entrepreneur, singer, public speaker, and educator. Originally from Snow Hill, NC Jelina is an inspirational advisee on topics such as good parenting, nurturing healthy relationships, and self-love. When she is not inside the classroom teaching mathematics, she can be found doing what she loves most. Singing and writing are two skills Jelina has been perfecting most of her life.

Jelina is a two time graduate of North Carolina A&T State University and member of Delta Sigma Theta Sorority, Inc. Upon receiving her B.S in Mathematics, she found herself and her life story being featured in media outlets such as Huffington Post, Today News, Popsugar, Fox News, The Shade Room, and many others. In 2017, Jelina and her son Karter, published their first co-written book, The Boy With No Shadow. This achievement was the career catapult for J. Sheppard. In October of 2018, J. Sheppard released her second book, "Overcoming A Breakup: A Lover's Guide To Resilience." This is her first publishing on healing and relationships and is indeed monumentally life changing.

J. Sheppard's purpose in life involves "overcoming heartbreaks for your heart's sake". Her latest release is helping lovers everywhere. Grab your copy today!

Just a Black Girl from Flint…In Corporate

Megan D. King

Human Resources is my chosen career. It's not what I attended college for, and it's not a field I was aware of as I graduated high school. Like many, I graduated from high school with an exact idea of what the next ten years would look like. College graduate by twenty-two. Financial stability and great career by twenty-three. Happily married by twenty-five. And welcoming my first child in our new home by twenty-eight. Then, I got to undergrad and realized there is a whole world out there I knew nothing about. There were many experienced to be had and lessons to learn. I walked across the stage as a college graduate with an extensive future ahead. If you're like me, you get your dream entry-level position in your chosen field, vow to work hard, set goals of moving up the corporate ladder, save money and invest, support your family, give back to your community, travel and conquer the world.

But what do you do if your dream job isn't a dream?

You hop on a plane, fly across the country and find your passion. At least that's what I did. That's how I found the career I love. I have worked at all levels of human resources. I am currently the HR leader at a national media and advertising company and a member of the senior leadership team. Each day, what drives me is the ability to help others identify their goals, work on personal and professional development, and create initiatives that not only meet organizational and revenue goals, but also positively impact the lives of team members.

Frequently, I encounter team members who are in some version of the same place that I was: needing a change, looking for more, or deciding what is next. It is my passion to assist them in investigating those questions and finding their passion. As my career progressed, I have gone from handling team member activities, and advocating for additional PTO days, to managing the strategy and vision of all people operations. From staffing budgets to multi-office pandemic plans and acquisition preparation, I am constantly looking to impact, not just the business, but team members in every way. I am passionate about the business, but even more so about the *people.*

I am always interested in what drives team members and other leaders. That interest includes insights, analytics and metrics; questions and solutions surrounding the "why"; identifying and evolving a culture of grit; and pushing team members across organizations to live out loud and be their true authentic selves. I partner with leaders, helping them to enrich and empower their team members.

But what happens when your own enrichment and empowerment comes to quick and hard halt?

Senior leadership team. Executive. Top of your department at your company. For some, when you hear those, it sounds like you've made it. Dreams realized, and nothing but up from there. But how do you continue to grow and move up, especially as a Black woman? How do you manage double standards, the "good ol' boys club," and inclusivity when you're a leader, but not included? Black women are currently the most educated demographic in the U.S. when you look at the number of associate's and bachelor's degrees earned. Black women are also amongst the fastest growing demographic of entrepreneurs in the U.S. But when you look at representation in the C-suite, there is a different narrative. Black women currently represent less than 1% of CEOs at Fortune 500 companies. From 2000 to 2020, there have only been 19 Black CEOs at Fortune 500 companies. Many people talk about glass ceilings. But how do you break them? Who teaches you the game? How do you help yourself? Do you really want to?

Corporate America definitely seems like a game with two separate sets of rules. Black women in corporate America are less likely to receive promotions or support and the necessary access to advance in their careers than their male or white colleagues. In my years working in corporate America, private, public and nonprofit sectors, I've worked roles from executive assistant to executive. In that time, and growing in Human Resources, I have seen many different things. There's always the good and bad, but it's the ugly that resonates. In all that I have experienced and seen, the one thing that I find applies across all roles, sectors and levels is that Black women have to put themselves first in their careers. It seems like the higher you climb the ladder, the further and more complicated each rung and the fewer people you have pulling you up. Sponsors and mentors become fewer, and politics become more widespread.

My older friends, aunts and uncles, and seasoned mentors from earlier in my career, told me to find a company, work hard, and move up the ranks. That dedication will pay off and politics can't stop your shine. I've decided to keep those things in mind, while also operating using a four-step doctrine. It's worked for me so far, and it fits many different situations.

Know Thy Self, Grow Thy Self

It can take a lot to bring your authentic self to work. But push past the ideal employee and show up as you. Who are you? What do you want? Realize that this is everchanging, and it's okay. Understanding yourself and having balance can provide you with extra insight into how to navigate and drive your career, as well as protect you from negative experiences and derailment. Knowing yourself, and knowing what you want, provides career development from a place that no one can tap into like you. You know what you want. Make sure you have the skills and tools needed to achieve, and go get it.

Have a Passion Plan

What is most important to you? What do you want your legacy to look like? What do you genuinely enjoy? These are questions that often lead back to your passion. Those who enjoy what they do, and excel at it, are usually working in a field or on something that they are passionate about. Corporate performance review meetings are usually riddled with questions about where you'd like to be in three years and what skills you'd like to obtain. That's not the plan we're talking here. What we're talking about is what makes you get up and go each day. What drives you? Identify it or those things, and start building a plan with goals and benchmarks to get there. Grinding in this area will keep you shining, inside and out.

Move in Silence

Social media. With your boss that you don't 100% trust. In circles that aren't tried and true. With whomever will listen, searching for validation. All places that, if possible, don't overshare. Often, it is better to spend less time talking about what you are planning to do and more time doing it. Moving in silence doesn't mean you can't get help from others, that you have to work on your goals all alone, or that you can't trust anyone in life. But being mindful of who you share with. The energy received, and who cheers you on, definitely impacts reaching the finish line. Execution is always at the top of the list.

Be Loyal ... to You, Not a Company

It feels great to excel at work, to have established tenure and to feel safe. But what job is really safe? Prioritize you and make decisions based on that. Keep your options open for opportunities. It's okay to always leave your LinkedIn on for "Open to Work." It's okay to interview sometimes just to understand the market and where you fall. Are you compensated equitably? Are you doing the job of three people at another company? Is there a company culture out there that affords you all of your current rewards and elevates you? Last, but not least, know when to exit. Prioritize dedication and hard, smart work for companies that are deserving. Prioritize opportunities that are mutually beneficial outside of just salary and benefits.

Start from this place when making decisions and begin the work. Whether in the corporate boardroom or a shared cubicle, if you have a corporate goal, follow it. Corporate America can be cutthroat and competitive. But you must always keep your brand at the forefront. Be diligent in your development and trajectory. Hold yourself accountable. But, don't forget to hold others accountable, too.

About Megan D. King

Megan D. King, SHRM-SCP, is a Human Resources professional passionate about people, strategy, and creative big picture approaches. Megan currently works within marketing, advertising and entertainment- Driving strategy, engagement, D&I, and leveraging HR for sustainable growth. At work, home and in her community, Megan's goal is to make an impact.

Megan recently joined Detroit's entrepreneurial scene with two business ventures- Royal Luxe Event Design, a boutique event planning company and Liquid Lush, a luxury mobile bartending company.

Megan consistently gives back via multiple community organizations with the Midnight Golf Program closest to her heart. Megan volunteers with the program, mentoring during the school year and annually chaperones a weeklong college tour inclusive of HBCU's.

Megan built her career foundation at non-profits and tech startups in the Bay Area, recently returning to Michigan. Megan is currently an MBA candidate at Michigan State University and member of Alpha Kappa Alpha Sorority, Inc.

You Got This, Precious!

Precious J. Bradley

In 2020, I found myself spiraling. I was alone, by myself with all of my thoughts. I was good in the beginning. I had been praying for a break. I needed some rest, some time to regroup and plan. I didn't realize how long it would be though. I knew from the beginning that this year, 2020, was going to be my turning point. My last year in my 20s. I spent a lot of time reflecting on what I had accomplished in those roaring 20s. I graduated from one of the top HBCUs in the country with honors. I got my degree! Something a lot of people from my hometown don't accomplish. I moved out of state, in total isolation, and just lived. I moved to Florida after graduation because I never thought I could live outside of my state. I knew this was a big step to break my small-town mindset. I published my first children's book. I started a career in education (which was not planned at all). And I started my own business, Precious Cargo Doula Services, LLC. In my 20s, I also accomplished something that, deep down, I knew was a long shot.

I found my biological parents.

I was abandoned as a two-week-old baby. I was left on a church daycare doorstep in a box with a blanket, a few diapers, and a sheet. It was a dark, cool, winter's morning before the sun rose. According to my biological mother, she waited for the police to come before she left the scene. I was discovered by a daycare worker. She thought someone had left a box of kittens. But it was me…whimpering and making the sweet, innocent sounds only a baby could make. After I was taken into custody, I was placed in the foster care system. From there, I was adopted by my parents, Ronald and Sheila Bradley.

Precious is the name my father gave me. My mother always wanted to be a mother. At an early age, she faced many health issues and, ultimately, had to get a hysterectomy, making it impossible for her to bear children. She always told me the story of how she lost her first little girl. I remember her being so vivid in her detail when she retold the story that it played in my mind like an episode of ER. After her hysterectomy, she never gave the dream up of being a mother. She married my father in 1982 and, in 1991, after my father returned from the war, they decided to expand their family. The deal was that if I was a girl, my mother would name me, Jaleesa, from her favorite character from her favorite TV show, "A Different World". Later in life right after my mother passed, I would meet the actress that portrayed this character, Dawn Lewis. If I was a boy, my father would name me. The deal went out the window when my father and I came face to face. They drove to Liberty, North Carolina from Jacksonville, North Carolina to pick me up. The only information they had was that there was a baby near Greensboro who was healthy and ready for a new home. When they arrived at my foster home, I was in a walker. I walked right up to my father and grabbed him on his leg. According to how the story has been told to me, my father, with tears in his eyes, turned to my mother and told her that he had to name me Precious.

"I want everyone in this world that crosses my path to know how precious she is to me."

pre·cious

/ˈpreSHəs/

adjective

(of an object, substance, or resource) of great value; not to be wasted or treated carelessly.

Symbolically, everything that led up to that moment would be the foundation of my purpose. It was the start of my full cypher journey. A journey I'm still traveling on today.

Fast forward to February 2018. After recently moving back to North Carolina, I told myself that this would be my last attempt at searching for my biological parents, at least for a while. I was approaching my late 20s, and felt I was using a lot of my energy toward this goal. A goal that many questioned if it was even in my best interest. Another part of me felt that this would be the last time I would need to search because this was my time. I don't know how to explain it. I just had my mind made up that I wasn't going to have to do this again. I went to my local news station and had them run the story (again). A month later, I got a hit on ancestry.com that would lead to my biological father, and ultimately, my biological mother.

With all the accolades and accomplishments I made throughout my 20s, I still felt empty. Finding my biological parents, and having that experience not reach my expectations, uncovered a lot of issues that I didn't address earlier, most of them being mental. My purpose in life shifted from "doing this to make my parents proud, make so and so happy, or because I am supposed to" to "I am doing what I want because I want to." I literally spent the quarantine period healing. I cried like a baby in a fetal position many nights in my bed, by myself, battling myself. The notorious imposter syndrome!

Am I good enough? Why don't they like me? Did I do something wrong? Am I going to get what I've always dreamed of? I'm almost 30 and ain't even close to starting a family like my friends. I don't like my job. Am I going to have to do this the rest of my life just to keep my bills paid? Is my health declining or am I super stressed? My thoughts kept me up at night and it became too much. I hired my therapist, who I now look at as my adopted auntie. (Please let me take a quick side bar moment to tell you that therapy is good. Don't ever let someone shame you for using these God-given services. Prayer without work is dead. This is part of the work…and you better WERK IT HUNTY.)

When you know your purpose, you live a meaningful life. First, you must discover what matters to you, without any outside influences. That's exactly what I did during lockdown. I started reading self-help books. I watched documentaries from people I looked up to. I created a self-love ritual and spoke positive affirmations to myself in my mirror. I wrote out everything I felt, good, bad and the ugly. This gave me a laser-sharp focus for moving ahead in my 30s. "We moving differently" is an understatement.

Every day, we face change. I had to let go of people, ideas and traditions that no longer served me. I had to come to grips with change.

Although it hurt for that moment, I knew it was for my better. I redirected the energy used to question others' motives to myself. Take one day at a time and live in the present moment. Set your goals and work toward them until you have accomplished them all! Once you shift your mindset, the universe shifts, as well. Every day brings its new challenges. But I feel more confident in my purpose now than I did last year (or just a few months ago). Let me be the example. It's okay to reinvent and rediscover your purpose at any given point in your life.

Setbacks are simply setups to make us stronger. You got this, precious.

"Lead me and guide me along the way. Lord if you lead me, I will not stray. Lord let me walk each day with thee. Lead me oh Lord, lead me."

About Precious J. Bradley

Precious J. Bradley, a product of adoption, was raised in Jacksonville, North Carolina by her two loving parents Ronald & Sheila Bradley. At a very young age Bradley expressed an interest in writing short stories and poems. She graduated from White Oak High School in 2009, and received her B.S in Journalism and Mass Communication with a concentration in Broadcast Production in 2013 from North Carolina A&T State University. Upon graduation, she moved to Jacksonville Florida to pursue a career in education. Bradley is the owner of Precious Cargo Doula Services, LLC, providing families support for positive birth experiences. She hopes to publish more books in the future that promote the love between women of all ages, while breaking learning barriers in the classroom. Bradley loves watching children develop, exploring nature/traveling, and learning history. Bradley currently resides in Greensboro, North Carolina where she works as an Educator and Birthing Doula.

My Soul Told Me to Go!

Sade Solánge Cooper

I graduated with my Bachelor of Arts degree in Mass Communications on May 19, 2010. By May 20, 2010, I was ready to enter the workforce. I had previously been employed by several retailers, a grocery outlet, ice cream parlor and GAP, Inc. At the time of graduation, I was working part-time for a car dealership on nights, weekends and holidays, with zero consistencies in my schedule. Though I performed exceptionally well with the company, I had a degree now, and I no passion for what I was doing. So, it was time for a change of scenery. Being a new graduate, the anticipation of receiving your first offer letter with your largest salary to date was exponentially high. But we were fresh out of an economic recession, and the job applications were being rejected left and right. Six years later, I was offered a job for a Marketing Coordinator position with an architecture firm in downtown L.A. Sounds fancy, huh? Hell, yeah! I accepted that Monday thru Friday, 9-to-5 opportunity, without hesitation. A week after being promoted at the car dealership, I submitted my two-week notice and packed my bags in preparation of my new career.

On day one, I noticed that I stood out like a pink porcupine at a petting zoo. I was the only Black woman in the building. On day two, I was involved in a bad car accident on my way to work, which delayed my onboarding process. When I returned, I learned how to access the company roster and view profile images of all 161 staff members across three locations. To my surprise, I was not only the only Black woman, but the only Black person and one of the youngest in the company. I didn't know whether I should have been impressed because "I had made the cut" or ashamed because I felt like an affirmative action hire. Nonetheless, my attitude remained the same: *I'll get the job done and try to open doors for others who look like me.*

Two months in, my attitude changed. *Oh, this definitely isn't for me. But what would I look like walking away so soon after hyping this new job up all over my social media accounts? Had enough time gone by for me to make a logical decision to part ways, or was I just being picky?* Many of my colleagues did not even speak or try to welcome me into the new environment. One of the firm's principals asked if I was "another new hire" because they thought I was a different person the day I came into work rocking a new hairstyle. I had taken my kinky twists out and wore my natural hair. It baffled me because I knew damn well that they didn't hire another Black woman before I'd finished my 90-day probation period. Adjusting was such a struggle. I felt like I was a part of an experiment at times.

Eventually, two more Black staff members were hired, but I still had absolutely nothing in common with 90% of the people I worked with. During virtual video meetings with my peers in the other offices, I felt like I was on display at a museum based on the way they looked at me. I felt as if they overly apologized for the smallest things, which they expected me to be irate and irrational over. Everything was awkward and uncomfortable, but still very new. I continued on the journey and managed to adopt new ways to adjust. One of my coping mechanisms was to over indulge in the snack drawer I created at my desk. I hardly ever got up and moved around because I was always drowning in deadlines and there weren't many places to walk to and return within the hour designated for lunch breaks. Further into my new position, I connected with one like-minded, professional woman who shared the same sentiments about the company and its culture. We became work besties. We ate lunch together three to four times a week. Once a month, we invited two other ladies in the office; they were of Asian and Caucasian descent, and my bestie was Mexican. I referred to us as the *Diversity Lunch Crew.*

In December of 2017, each person in the office participated in a Secret Santa gift exchange. At this point, I had had enough interactions with my co-workers to purchase a nice gift for the person's name I selected. I wanted to make sure that he opened it and knew I put thought into it. Ideally, that's the way it should've worked out when everyone opened their present. Everyone except *me! What the hell am I supposed to do with this shit?* I thought while I pretended to be appreciative. *Of all the things to give a person you don't know personally—a scarf, gift card, fleece blanket, movie tickets—I get a damn Architecture 101 book.* It was similar to a book for dummies. Coming from the sarcastic, arrogant individual who gave it to me, it was an insult.

Receiving that book made me realize what type of environment I worked in. It was dull and unfit for my spirit. These people spent half of their day sending me emails, requesting marketing information and asking for my creative or technical assistance to make them look good on their projects. They spent 50+ hours a week roaming the same halls, sitting on the same damn toilet seats, and sharing appliances in the kitchen with people they never acknowledged and/or had the decency to get familiar with. I was 'people.' It was almost as if I was invisible until someone needed me. I noticed how they engaged with each other. I never had the same social experiences. I made one genuine connection in an office full of human beings I saw more than my family and friends combined. How do you interact so frequently with someone for eighteen months and never even learn how to pronounce their first name correctly? One of my coworkers didn't even try. Whether he knew it or not, he was my least favorite person in the office. I know it bothered him that I corrected him every single time he mispronounced my name. No, buddy! You will not repeatedly approach my desk with, *"Hey, can you?"* to avoid saying, *"Hello, Sade"* first.

Of the 161 employees in the company, over 60% were White men. Of the 61 people in the office, 90% went to architectural school, never left their desks, and ate building designs for breakfast. They did not speak to you as you passed by in the hall or stood behind them in the printer room. They did not thank you for ordering lunch and dessert or for dropping off birthday trinkets on their desks. I never did anything for recognition because I kept the same energy throughout my time with the company, despite my kind gestures being overlooked. I just wanted everyone to feel like someone in that place cared about them because I never felt that way. Hell, one day someone had the nerve to send me an email and ask me to refill the paper towel in the bathroom because I suppose my "token black girl role" was "the help", even though everyone had access to the storage closet to replenish supplies themselves.

By the middle of February 2018, every day was a battle. I spent many moments suppressing my inner-G clap backs in person and holding a tight grip on my Black Twitter fingers via email exchanges to avoid conflict and confrontation. I tried not to roll my eyes and to exercise patience with my colleagues. But the microaggressions, and bold displays of the company's *White is right* culture, were sending signals to my soul. I had to go. I resigned approximately twenty months into my employment.

I walked away with my head held high, but without an exit plan.

Being uncomfortable and feeling invisible every day forced me into building my own table. I compiled lists of my skills and passions, in addition to writing down what I desired in exchange for what I had to offer. I made the mistake of chasing a higher salary, better schedule and impressive-sounding title. But this experience taught me that those things were insignificant. In May of 2018, I invested my time and energy into growing my event planning business, Sade Cooper Events, and became an independent contractor for an event/photography/film studio. I have met some of the most amazing people and have enjoyed the flexibility of a schedule that I decide for myself. I freed up more time because my morning commute and workdays weren't as long. With those extra hours, I took on various gigs that have continuously funded more of my passions. Since I let go, I've maintained a loss of twenty-seven pounds. I have the financial stability I need, and I am in the process of publishing my first book.

Listen to your soul when it tells you to go!

About Sade Solánge Cooper

Sade Solánge Cooper is a creative writer, storyteller and event planner. An Inglewood, Ca native, she developed a passion for writing early on, having published her first piece in an anthology of poetry by the age of eight. Encouraged by her educators, close friends and family members to share her work, she began participating in slam poetry tours across Los Angeles reciting her poetry in book stores and coffee shops alongside local poet legends. Sade would later start a blog in 2014.

Sade received her undergraduate degree in Mass Communications from California State University, Dominguez Hills. When she is not writing, Sade is coordinating and managing events for clients, traveling, enjoying some form of music entertainment and giving back to the homeless population via donations and volunteer service with local non-profit organizations. She is working on her first published novel to be released in the fourth quarter of 2021.

A Million-Dollar Contract

Susan Gaddy Pope

The last thing I wanted to do was *teach.* I just wanted to *dance.* I had enjoyed a few years performing and working in fashion and textiles. But when the home division of Burlington Industries folded, I was faced with unemployment for the first time in my life. I didn't know what to do. My mom, who was a retired educator, suggested I try substitute teaching until I figured out what I wanted to do with my life. I was a horrible test taker. So, I figured if I didn't study for the test, I'd fail, and that would be the end of the story. Guess what? I passed!

With a substitute license in hand, I reluctantly proceeded to the district office to receive my assignment. With no pedagogy experience, and a major attitude, I approached the HR director and asked for a kindergarten or first grade class. Those classes had to be easy. The HR director, without even looking at my resume, said, "I don't have a job for a kindergarten teacher, but I have a job for a dance teacher. Can you dance?" Talk about divine intervention! I had been dancing since I was six. I'd obtained my BA in dance performance, but never intended to teach dance.

Working for the NYC Department of Education proved to be a lifesaver. Not only did I prepare numerous students for entrance into NYC's specialized high schools, but I also discovered the joy of teaching in an urban setting. After having my son, I went on to obtain my master's degree in dance education. The dance studio became a lab of discovery for my students and myself. Together, we explored new ways of moving, connected to historical figures, and created dances that were transformative. I thought I was happy, but something was eating away at my self-esteem. It took a while for me to recognize that I was in an emotionally abusive marriage. It wasn't bad every day. I figured it would get better, but it just kept getting worse. By the end, I was emotionally wounded, and I had lost my sense of self.

I packed up my son and we left.

Life as a single mom had its fair share of challenges, but the biggest challenge was commuting back and forth between New York and New Jersey. The divorce had taken a toll on both of us but thank God for my village. I had a great support system. But still, I knew I needed to be closer to my son.

The much-anticipated phone call came late one Friday afternoon in August, a month before school was to begin. I had been offered a position teaching dance in my community. Elated, I felt like life's pendulum was swinging in my favor. My first day of work, September 11, 2001, I dropped my son off at school, something I hadn't been able to do before. After my divorce, I had to rely on my village, a small circle of friends and my church family, to get him to school and to pick him up. This was a new day for both of us. After dropping him off, I drove a few blocks away to my new school. My first class came into my dance studio at 8:40. I was so excited to introduce Mr. Linwood's fifth-grade class to the world of dance. Within ten minutes, the world changed.

Mr. Sanchez, the music teacher, came into my classroom at 8:50 a.m. to tell me that a plane had crashed into The World Trade Center. I didn't believe him. I simply continued with the opening of my lesson. At about 9:15, Mr. Linwood came to pick up his class early. He told me a second plane had crashed into The World Trade Center. Suddenly, I realized something was deathly wrong. I could hear sirens outside, but I couldn't see anything. There were no windows in the classrooms. When I interviewed for this position over the summer, I hadn't even noticed the absence of windows. There was no computer in my room, so I felt totally disconnected from the rest of the world.

After my morning classes, I finally got a chance to talk to someone. The security guard confirmed The World Trade Center attacks. Parents came to the school in droves to pick up their children. My thoughts quickly turned to my own child. I called Spencer's school and they reassured me he was fine, so I stayed put. Once the school day was over, I just wanted to hug my child. I rushed to Spencer's school, only to find out he was not there. Someone had come to pick him up. I panicked. *Where was my child?* As far as I knew, his father was not in town, so it couldn't have been him. Fear has a way of paralyzing you and making you think the worst. I called around to all my friends who normally would pick him up for me as needed. No one had seen him. I didn't know what else to do.

I went to my church, which was just a few blocks away, to pray and solicit help. When I walked into the church, there was Spencer, sitting, doing his homework. The afterschool program, which Spencer had been a part of for years, had picked him up, thinking I still worked in New York. I quickly updated all my information, thanked them, and took Spencer home. We watched the day's events on the news. I felt an immense sense of grief and sadness for all those who lost their lives that day.

The next few years at my new school were challenging. The district, which had been under state control since 1995, was focused on test scores. There were fights in the school every day. I experienced a high turnover rate of students. I saw children removed from school by family services. The school often went into lockdown whenever there was gun activity outside. I had my pocketbook stolen by a student's mother while her child was performing on stage. I didn't feel like I was making a difference in these students' lives. If I wasn't making a difference, what was the point in being here? I felt powerless, unappreciated and ill-prepared to service these students. My feelings of inadequacy and low self-esteem resurfaced. I contemplated leaving education. One night, I seriously began to weigh my options. I prayed and asked God for a sign to help me know what to do. The next morning, I woke up and decided to open Facebook, which I had recently joined. When I logged on, there was a message from a former student of mine from New York.

The message read:

"Ms. Greene", (that was my name before I remarried) "I have been looking for you. You may remember me as Jeffrey Miranda, but I use a stage name now. You were my dance teacher at I.S. 218. I wasn't the best student, but you never gave up on me. You

always believed I was talented and told me to always reach for my dreams. I wanted to thank you for the discipline you taught me through dance. I just signed a million-dollar signing contract and I attribute it to the discipline necessary for the arts. I am grateful and I just wanted to say thank you."

I sat at the computer, reading the message over and over again, with tears in my eyes. I realized God had answered my prayers. It was not time for me to leave education. I had asked God for a sign the night before. Jeffrey showed up with a big, bold sign. I tried to remember what, and how exactly, had I taught Jeffrey that gave him this level of discipline.

My lessons in New York were not centered on teaching discipline. Nor were they centered on producing great dancers. They were centered on teaching the concepts and elements of dance, which mirrored life. I went to school that morning with a different perspective. Before Jeffrey's message, I had allowed the unfortunate incidents that had occurred over the years to shift my perspective. I had distanced myself from my students as a means of masking my own feelings. Now I understood why I was feeling inadequate. I had failed to operate in a truly authentic manner. The negative experiences in the school were all too reminiscent of the emotions I harnessed at the end of my marriage. In order for me to make a difference, I had to change my own mindset. I reached down deep to find the enthusiasm I carried with me at the beginning of the day on September 11, 2001.

I pressed the reset button, got my joy back, and gave my students the best version of myself. From there, I saw a change. Jeffrey's message helped me to not only recommit myself to educating my students in a way that was affirming and transformative, but to also trust God's purpose for me. Jeffrey reminded me to never give up on myself, my students, nor their families. Transformation takes time and commitment. If I could just keep pushing, each of my students and I would have full access to a million-dollar contract.

About Susan Gaddy Pope

Susan Pope holds a BA in dance from the University of Maryland and a MA in dance education from Teachers College, Columbia University. She is an Arnhold Fellow in the dance education doctoral program at Teachers College, Columbia University. 2017 Susan created I DANCE BECAUSE, a nonprofit organization dedicated to dance education, scholarship and the emotional healing aspects of dance. Her publications include: an article in Dance Education in Practice titled TEACHING DANCE HISTORY TO MIDDLE SCHOOL STUDENTS, I DANCE BECAUSE..., a collection of stories, essays and poems about dance; DANCING MY PRAYERS, a guide to combining movement and prayer in your devotional life; an article in the International Journal of AAHPERD titled *Mourning Into Dancing – The Transformation of Lives: A personal Journey;* May of 2000, Susan was invited to the White House to speak at a conference titled *Raising Responsible and Resourceful Youth.*

Complexity of the Strong Black Woman

Tanisha Markland

For as long as I could remember, I have always been told I am a "very strong" woman. That's something most black women are often labeled as. Black and strong. Quite often, both of these traits dictate how we are treated, which forces many of us to tolerate and overcome a certain type of treatment—not only from society—but from other women, as well. All because we are trying to uphold the image of a "strong black woman".

At this point in my life, I have accepted the description. Not, because of what society defines a "strong woman" as but, what I define a "strong woman" as. For a long time, it was hard for me to see myself the way others saw me. I focused a lot on others, my personal struggles and shortcomings. I did my best not to show my flaws. For many years, I was struggling to stay afloat. I felt I was drowning in many aspects of my life. I found the strength so many people talked about the moment I reflected on the things I had overcome.

The Strong Black Mother

My mother suffered for three long years from duodenal cancer. Throughout those years, we created amazing memories and had life-changing conversations. Despite the circumstances, we enjoyed our drives into the city three times a week to Memorial Sloan Kettering Hospital. We motivated each other at the gym and relaxed in the house on the days she could barely get out of bed. We bonded in a way that we never did before because life forced us to do so. Years went by, and things got worse. I started to realize how short life could be because of the possibility of her not being with me. I sat beside her every day in hospice care as they "made her comfortable." One evening after work, I walked into her hospital room and watched as she typed on an imaginary computer and looked at an imaginary screen. When I asked her what she was doing, she told me she was getting things in order for her boss and arranging her funeral. Her response was devastating. I watched as she fell asleep and left, with my heart aching. The tightness in my chest, and the feeling in my stomach, led to uncontrollable tears.

I slid down the wall outside of the elevator a few steps away from her room. I made it no further than my car that night. I slept in the parking lot of the hospital. If that night wasn't enough, I woke up to a call from her oncologist, telling me it was time to increase her morphine. To cheer me up, he told me about how she was all smiles this particular morning because she thought we were going to take one of our regular rides to the city. I forced a chuckle so I would not cry. I thought about that ride to the city we wouldn't be able to take again.

I knew that, mentally, she was no longer present. I had a limited amount of time to enjoy her presence. I left the hospital parking lot with my flawless public façade to go arrange the funeral.

The next morning, before I got dressed to go see her, I received the phone call telling me my mother had passed away. What I thought would be at least a week with the increase in morphine was only twenty-four hours.

I opted for a closed casket because, for two out of the three years that she fought cancer, she did not want anyone to see her. At the funeral, I stood up and read the eulogy I wrote. I did not shed a tear. That wasn't because I was strong. It was because I wanted to display the strength everyone told me I had. I saw no benefit in showing my vulnerability amongst the people I loved. I had to be strong for them. Similar to my mother, I needed to make it seem like I had it all together at all times. When, realistically, I was in pain mentally, emotionally and physically. The night of my mother's funeral, I went to a basketball game in my hometown to clear my mind. One of my favorite things to do is to watch children in their element. Children are always my reminder that there is a future and I needed that. Those hours brought me a moment of joy. From that night on, life just passed by until my next reality check.

More than Survival

In August of 2018, four years and two months after my mother had passed away, I cried with a patient in the front office of my job. She was twenty-eight years old like me. She had just found out that she was cancer-free. At that moment, I gave myself permission to cry. I knew people would only look at my tears as empathy for the patient's survival, not as the tears from the pain I had bottled up for over four years because my mother did not survive. At this moment, reality set in. I was surviving, but that's all I was doing. I needed to deal with myself. No matter what it took, I needed to do more than just survive.

I made the choice to quit my job. I was honest with the manager when I told her I could no longer settle. Even though it was Tuesday, my last day would be the upcoming Friday. The manager and human resources called me for weeks after to offer me more of everything—besides what I needed. Once I made the decision to leave that job, I had to learn how to be comfortable with being uncomfortable by reflecting on every aspect of my life. I went to counseling to adjust to the changes. Gradually, my perspective on vulnerability changed. That vulnerability was my newfound strength.

Why did I settle for so long? Simply because I put value on false security. The false security that I received from plenty of jobs that gave me a raise or reward to make me feel valued. The false security that I looked for from society that made me think it was best to make it look good, when I really wasn't good. False security in toxic relationships that I allowed because of companionship. I used to settle in life because I watched many people around me settle, and they seemed to be okay. Maybe some of them lacked the information. Maybe others lacked the drive. But, as for me, I lacked neither one. I was just making excuses because of my fear to step into the unknown. I didn't want to fail. I thought that because I am that strong black woman, it would hurt my image to have to show that failure.

Now I know my strength was built through all the vulnerable moments. My experiences taught me that success is subjective. I am now aware of my life's purpose, and I am intentional about living in my purpose. My mother's death was out of my control, as are many things that happen in life. What I can control is my mindset. For too long, I allowed full-time jobs to be a distraction. That moment I had after my mother's funeral, when I chose to watch children in their element, I chose to be in my element. I now choose the service of children and their families over false security. I know the future I want. I know the difference I want to make. I finally understand and appreciate the process of personal growth.

There is a saying, "When the student is ready, the teacher will appear." It wasn't until I was ready that I was clear on what I had to do. I went back to get an additional degree in Education because I realized I always had a passion for working with children. I know the importance of a good foundation, and I needed the basics to create my brand. The Influential Brand. A brand that focuses on education through exploration. I did not grow up in a traditional way. I have an appreciation for the non-traditional approach to many things in life, especially education. Children need guidance and exposure in safe spaces to learn about themselves from an early age. Once a person learns about themselves, and their value, they have the ability to believe in their greatness.

Now that I am clear on my calling, it's liberating. Self-reflection is self-love. Making a difference requires strength and discipline. I reflected on my past and found my purpose. I live by Maya Angelou's quote, "If you get, give. If you learn, teach." I am a strong black woman, but those are just a few words that can be used to describe me. I am not defined by, nor am I confined to, the box that society tries to put the Black woman in.

Message for the Black Queen

Be still and reflect often. Life happens. Many things are out of our control. Accept that! Control the things you can control. Don't get in your own way by allowing everything to get in the way. Whatever it is you're searching for, hoping for, or praying for, take the first step necessary. Keep in mind that fear is false evidence appearing real. It's important to know that God orders our steps. God's plan is always better than our own. A positive mindset leads to a positive life. Always be true to you!

About Tanisha Markland

Tanisha Markland was born and raised in Westchester County, New York. She received multiple degrees throughout her years of education and views her degree in Childhood education as the most valuable because it aligns with her purpose. She is a Dual- Certified Educator. Her certifications are in Elementary School Education and Early Childhood Special Education. Her entrepreneurial journey has taken her beyond the classroom environment generating multiple streams of income and coaching others through some of the processes she has taken.

She is the Founder of the "Influential" Brand. This brand consists of a travel business that specializes in multi-generational travel and a non-profit organization for children ages 8-18. She's inspired by the children in this world and deliberate about being a lifelong learner. Her life's work is to educate those around her by being an example, providing opportunities and the space to explore life.

Failed Plans...Regroup and Go Again

TaQiyyah Floyd

"What do you want to be when you grow up?"

Everyone, at some point, always asks, or gets asked, that question. I despise that question now. Many people asked if I wanted to be a teacher. I never wanted to work in the school system. In fourth grade, I "decided" I wanted to be a professional basketball player overseas. I've had the travel bug since childhood. First, I would attend college to become a labor and delivery nurse, thanks to watching Birth Stories on the TLC network. Then, I'd go into that field after retiring from playing basketball. I wish the question was worded differently to consider that the backup plan sometimes needs two or three additional backup plans. The question should be something like, "How many different career fields do you want to try in your lifetime?"

I went through the majority of my life thinking I'd found what I was meant to be. When I reached for that basketball and nursing door, they were both shut in my face. My university's basketball coach at the time said, "You're too quiet to be a point guard." In my head, I didn't understand what that had to do with my ability to play the game. I should have said something then. Say everything you're thinking please!

In nursing, I passed my labs. But I got two Ds in lecture. I wasn't genuinely happy about walking across the graduation stage because I knew I didn't know what was next for me, like my peers who are business owners, paralegals, educators, accountants and engineers. I didn't know God at the time. So, my anxiety was heightened. Negative thoughts and fake smiles took over. I even tried to go into the military, but I failed the officers test by four points. I had no clue what to do!

Jobless for about a year, discovering this real world of adulting hits differently. I started applying to anything and everything. Still nothing. The Most High pulled on my heart strings. I learned about Him and who I am in Him. That year of feeling inadequate became my favorite year of spiritual growth. Reading my Bible, going to church, watching YouTube videos about God, listening to podcasts, and writing helped change my mindset. I still don't know what He specifically wants me to do. But spiritually, I know He made me a fighter.

I literally remember punching at a demon in my sleep attack one night. It was living in the physical world where I was trying to keep my head above water. Honestly, sometimes I'm still like, "Dang, Most High! Can I have some floaties?! I'm not doing so hot with this free-choice." Nevertheless, I started thinking about everything I'm interested in and everything I would be open to accomplishing if He allowed it. I made a list. It's long, but the possibilities are endless! I really enjoy helping other people. I like knowing people see me as trustworthy, dependable and caring. Yet again, there are roadblocks in society where no one wants to train you for your job, but they expect you to have years of experience. Having one job shows stability and that you're knowledgeable. Today, a 401k and benefits are deemed most valuable. I want the benefits package with bonuses. Who doesn't? However, I want to wake up every morning excited, not bored.

I worked in the school system for four years and actually enjoyed it! I loved my AU (autism) team and students, even after saying I would never work in the school system. I know. Never say, "Never." The problem was I felt stuck, like there were no opportunities to grow, without having to sell a kidney to go back to school. I don't know about you, but I'm ready to see what an environment not centered around greed looks like. As time progressed, I saw ESL ads and people who were ESL teachers as suggested friends on Instagram. I also came across Oxford Seminars. They were holding affordable courses at UNCC. So, I prayed and went for it. I came out with TEFL/TESOL certification (Teaching English as a Foreign Language/Teaching English to Speakers of Other Languages) and a lifelong recruiting oversees teaching service. I gave my top five locations to the recruiting team. They were South Korea, Japan, Thailand, Vietnam and Spain.

I got asked a lot by locals and foreign co-workers why I came to

Japan. Apparently, anime, a spouse and safety are the leading reasons for foreigners. South Korea also gave me an offer, which was way better, at least on paper. I asked God and, days later when I wasn't thinking about it, He gave me quite a few confirmations. That's why I selected Japan. It was really difficult at first living there. I knew little about the culture and people, other than what I observed when I visited the Americanized prefectures (Tokyo and Okinawa) of Japan two years before I knew I would actually be living there. My company had me in an older traditional area of Japan in Aichi prefecture. So, it was way different, but good. I had to overcome being homesick. I had to overcome the language barrier and using public transportation to and from all my different work locations (ten different schools). I had to overcome working non-stop and more, all during a global pandemic!

Being homesick was an experience. Once it hit me, I decided to learn how to make videos and make a YouTube channel. I also figured out my work routine and became interested in learning jiu-jitsu. I found a dojo, did a trial lesson and loved it. I joined immediately. I would get off work at 7 p.m. and happily hop into my kimono from 8 to 10 p.m. at least three to five times a week for ten months. It was all in Japanese, but I think me being naturally athletic helped a lot with picking the jiu-jitsu moves up easily. Definitely one of my best decisions, relieving stress through jiu-jitsu, writing, YouTube and talking to God is what helped me overcome all of my difficulties in Japan.

Today, I'm working toward getting in the door of as many professions as I can until God calls and says that's it. My goal is to have five to ten titles that I enjoy that may not have anything to do with each other. But they will yield multiple streams of passive income or offer joyful, free labor! I recently just signed up for doula training to see if that's a path I'd enjoy.

Many people characterize themselves by what they do. People say, "I'm a doctor. I'm a fitness trainer. I'm an artist. I'm an airman. I'm the manager at Chick-fil-A. I may not know my one "purposed" career role, but I know the type of woman I am and desire to be. A friend of mine told me about a devotional she was reading that said, "It's all about perspective." It's not the occupation that matters; it's the driving force.

The example she gave me was about three third grade teachers. When asked to describe what they do, the first teacher said, "I'm just teaching." The second teacher said, "I'm teaching science to kids." The third teacher said, "I'm preparing my students for not only fourth grade science, but for the world, through science and all the various opportunities it can provide."

Hearing the response of the third teacher, I immediately thought of Ms. Frizzle from The Magic School Bus. Only a crazy person wouldn't want to be in her class, whether you like science or not! It was the same question and same job, but all of them had significantly different outlooks. If you don't learn anything else from this book, or my chapter, join me in remembering the word perspective. I'm working on becoming a better woman and not allowing my subconscious feelings to have the upper hand. Instead, I am doing things that make me happy and give me peace, no matter how big or small.

Thanks for reading my TEDx Talk. I'm TaQiyyah Floyd, and I'm trying to live a full, adventurous life, while still figuring things out.

About TaQiyyah Floyd

TaQiyyah Floyd is an educator and aspiring author who can't help but to write novels for text messages. A woman that loves all movie genres except for horror, playing sports or any physical fitness activity and helping people. She claims Mitchellville, Maryland and Charlotte, North Carolina where she currently resides as home. In 2013 she graduated with a bachelor of science degree from North Carolina A&T State University. Her most recent accomplishment to date was the opportunity to work and live in Japan.

She believes answering the question of what do you want to be should come with several responses. Why not be a combination of all the things you enjoy? You can be the lawyer, the baker and an artist. The idea of acquiring jobs within her multiple interests and finding her way to accomplishing various things while enjoying life is her primary focus.

Falling in Love with My Purpose

Tiara Swain

Wow! This is an amazing opportunity to share how God revealed my purpose. Sharing my story like this is completely out of my comfort zone. So I appreciate you taking the time to learn more about my personal and professional journey. God revealed to me that my purpose in life is to love God and His people at all times.

In our darkest hours, God gives us the strength to push through or remove the challenge. Obstacles are lessons waiting to be revealed. The first obstacle I faced was at birth. I was born on February 14, 1993 prematurely at the University of Pennsylvania Hospital, weighing only 3 ½ lbs. Feeding tubes and ear surgeries were the norm. Like many families, I grew up in a single parent home in Philadelphia. Dad won custody of me and my older sister. There was never a dull moment in our house, especially when Dad learned how to cook. I still remember that chicken and detergent incident! My father worked three jobs, like a true Jamaican that he is. He never missed any moments. We lived four blocks away from my grandparents' house, so it was always a place to visit frequently in Germantown. My grandma said I was going to be different. Her exact words were, "Something is special about you Tiara. What five-year-old refuses to eat dinner until their homework is done?" I wanted to read books and attend museums, while my sister wanted to go to the mall. That was us for sure, oil and vinegar. But I am fortunate to have her in my corner always.

My father was highly active in his fraternity. So, volunteering at homeless shelters and for the Special Olympics were normal activities. At the Special Olympics, I passed out sports beverages and directed the athletes away from the field. One week later, my dad started asking questions about my responsibilities. I didn't remember all the details. This conversation changed my life. The next day, he purchased a laptop and explained the purpose of a resume. I was ten years old with a resume for school and volunteer work.

From second to the eighth grade, I was placed in the Mentally Gifted (MG) Program, where children are given tasks to commensurate with their academic work. It was a safe space to hide from students who teased me. You can't put a price on peace. I spent years learning scholastic information to win academic competitions. Likewise, my father married my stepmother, and I gained another sister and brother.

Having an absent mother presented an ongoing hindrance. Over time, feelings evolved from joy and happiness to disappointment and resentment toward her. I was envious of friends who had better relationships with their mothers. She missed birthdays, holidays and graduations—all of the important moments you would expect a parent to attend. Our conversations were filled with paranoia, and I felt torn. How could I feel so much disdain for someone I also loved?

In the eighth grade, three students were accepted into Central High School from my elementary school. I was the only female. This prestigious high school preps students to excel in college and life endeavors. This was another obstacle. I wasn't ranked at the top, and I was out of my comfort zone. I asked my dad for guidance on how to stand out. He told me the best way was to gain internship experience in high school and college. By the time I graduated college, I'd have years of experience. I learned so much completing management, marketing, and IT at UPenn and Johnson & Wales University. I gained exposure to brands like Starbucks, Marriot and Perelman Quadrangle.

When I was fifteen, I dated my first boyfriend. He was a tall, handsome football player. Two weeks after my sixteenth birthday, he invited me over his house. That night was different. His parents weren't home, and he sexually assaulted me. After it happened, I felt ugly and developed an eating disorder. A few months later, my best friend noticed something different about my face. The dermatologist diagnosed me with vitiligo, an autoimmune disease where cells are unable to produce enough melanin that causes areas of the skin to lose color. Stress magnifies this condition. This crucial event revealed that obstacles also come in several forms. This took a toll psychologically, mentally and physically.

I was not brave enough to disclose the information. So focusing all my time on schoolwork was the best way I dealt with the pain. In 2010, I was accepted into the International Baccalaureate Program, a vigorous advanced placement program. For the next two years, I had the same classes with the same people. I graduated with an International Diploma and Bachelor of Arts Degree, entering college with thirty credits. During undergraduate, I completed three business internships, served as Black Student Union President, and was the Vice President of the undergraduate chapter of my sorority.

The Black Student Union hosted an event called Sleeping Bag Weekend, an opportunity for high school students to stay at a college for the weekend. I was paired with a mentee and learned that she was also sexually assaulted. It all it made sense. I have to *love God's people.* Positive Patty and Princess were nicknames I earned because I was so happy all the time. Everything was perfect at school, until the day *after* my graduation. My International Finance Professor waited to post the grades and failed fifteen graduating seniors. My grade was a 69.6. On paper, I technically could not graduate. I had my first job on the line at Pepsi. God is such a provider. The dean found a discrepancy with my transcript and cleared me to receive that International Business Degree. That was God's grace for sure. Only He can move mountains like that.

I bombed the first interview at Pepsi. It was a panel, and I was so intimidated. Two weeks later, HR asked me to interview for a new role. It was the perfect fit, and I was promoted later that year. At the same time, I earned my MBA in management and was promoted. After one year, employees in good standing qualify to apply for a promotion. Unfortunately, one year turned into 3 ½ years in the same position. I applied to ten positions and was denied each time. *What was the disconnect? Performance wasn't an issue.* Management was complacent. HR shared the limited opportunities available. At this point, I was ready for change.

Within three weeks, I relocated to Atlanta to work at Kelly Services, an international staffing firm. Flesh decisions come with fleshly consequences. After spending time in this role, it was evident that I was far from happy. But I performed well. Out of frustration, I started a consulting firm that flopped. During this time, I reconnected with my biological mother, and learned that she was diagnosed with schizophrenia and currently homeless in Washington D.C. The anger disappeared and my perspective of her was forever altered. My focus shifted to provide as much support to her as possible. That same week, my first boyfriend finally apologized for the assault.

In Atlanta, I joined a church that July and was baptized in September. My walk with God became stronger. I stopped asking for things I wanted to happen. Changing my prayer to ask God to send me where He wanted me to be honored Him greater. One week later, I received a message from a recruiter, stating that my skills and background aligned with an account management role at LinkedIn in Chicago. Receiving that offer confirmed my purpose is to love God. Loving God means you're obedient to the process and that you fully trust the process. I was definitely out of my comfort zone, but I consistently surpassed each quota. Likewise, I joined the black ERG group as the Community Partnerships Lead, where I had the opportunity to impact schools and start new initiatives to push for diversity and inclusion.

In August of 2020, I successfully launched my consulting firm, Swain Solutions, which specializes in career coaching and business consulting. After helping a single mom land her first role with benefits, I realized this is the impact I want to have on the world. COVID created an opportunity for me to support individuals who were impacted by layoffs and business owners who were launching new ventures. God is so intentional, and this is only the beginning! Obstacles aren't meant to defeat us. They are opportunities to direct us closer to God. They are necessary for growth, and they challenge us to make better decisions.

About Tiara Swain

Tiara Swain is a Career and Business Consultant who helps professionals and startups build a competitive online presence by implementing tailored nctworking and branding strategies.

Before launching her consulting firm, Swain Solutions, in August 2020, Tiara has 6 years of experience in increasing revenue, reducing expenses, and developing brand strategies for Fortune 500 companies, including Enterprise Holdings, PepsiCo, Kelly Services, and LinkedIn.

Currently at LinkedIn, she is a Relationship Manager that enhances recruiting and branding strategies for 140 staffing firms. Likewise, Tiara serves as Pillar Lead for Community Partnerships for the Black Inclusion Group 's Chicago Office. In 2021, she won the Diversity, Inclusion, and Belonging Award for her work and community achievements.

Personally, Tiara Swain is an active member of Zeta Phi Beta Sorority, Incorporated, Mu Xi Zeta Chapter and leads finance workshops at her church, Fellowship Chicago. She enjoys skydiving, cooking, and listening to jazz music.

Embrace Change...It Leads to Purpose

Uniqua Quillins

In 2006, I realized what I possibly wanted to do with my life. I was in middle school, and I was only twelve years old. I loved sports. I was especially fond of ESPN analyst, Stephen A. Smith, and his show, *Quite Frankly.* He interviewed my favorite basketball player on that show, Allen Iverson. I was overly excited for this episode because, in a way, I felt Iverson and I were similarly misunderstood at times. I watched, intently, how Smith gave Iverson the platform to clear the air and pull back the curtain on some of the misconceptions about him. Then, it hit me! At the tender age of twelve, I said to myself, "That's what I want to do. I want to help people tell their stories!"

I said to myself, "I'm going to be the female version of Stephen A. Smith!"

So, I started chasing that dream! In middle school, I started by interviewing the minor league baseball team in my hometown of Beloit, Wisconsin. I also created stories for our middle school newspaper. In high school, I was a sports reporter. I later served as sports editor both my junior and senior years of school. I continued to chase the dream once I left for college at North Carolina A&T State University. I was a sports reporter, and I even wrote a front-page story about our basketball team winning the MEAC Championship in 2013.

Fast forward to my senior year at North Carolina A&T. I landed my first job in the television industry. I became an associate producer for WXII12 News in Winston-Salem, North Carolina. As I matriculated at North Carolina A&T, I realized I didn't want to be in front of the camera anymore. I wanted to create. So, landing this job right as I started my senior year of college was big for me. That job opened the door for me to become a news producer in Fort Myers, Florida. I had some great times career wise in Florida, along with some extremely challenging ones. I questioned why I was even in the news industry.

Through it all, I prevailed and made it to one of my dream markets – Charlotte, North Carolina.

God blessed me to not only be able to land a job in one of my dream markets, but at the number one station in the market: WSOC-TV. As I headed to Charlotte, everything felt like it was coming together.

Then, something shifted.

In November of 2019, two months after I started my new producing position in Charlotte, I noticed some of the same characteristics I displayed while working in Florida resurface. Because of the baneful environment I endured in Florida, I would do things like sit in my car for a long time to gather the strength to go into work. When I realized that mannerism came back, I timidly tapped into those emotions. I couldn't ignore them this time around. I couldn't blame the environment. It was something deeper. I realized it.

I didn't want to do news anymore.

It was very scary for me to admit that. To know that you've worked hard to achieve something, realize you don't love what you do, is a hard pill to swallow. It was as if I'd put myself in this box. I told myself that I'd started in news, so I had to stay in news forever. That is not the case! I believe God brought me to Charlotte to show me that. To show me the sky is limit and to show me that Philippians 4:13 is really true – I can do all things through Christ, not just what I received a degree in.

The coronavirus pandemic hit just as I was starting to accept that this would be my last stop in news. This was a blessing in disguise because it was during this time that I was able to do more research about what I really wanted to do. My eyes were opened to the fact that I could lead communications teams for major companies and be part of a bigger vision to push movements forward.

As my interest piqued from all the possibilities, my hard feelings toward working in news grew stronger. It got to the point where I was neglecting my job, just going through the motions, and doing the bare minimum. I was ready to leave. God used one of my co-workers to pull me back together. She told me, "You need to speak up more. You're here, so take up space." I received that wisdom and realized I can't be so focused on my next that I neglect operating in the blessing I'm standing in right now. There are still lessons to be learned that I will take into my next when it's time to make that move.

If you don't take anything else away from this chapter, know that change is inevitable, but it's not a bad thing. It's aligning us for our God-given purpose. Remember to operate in your blessing. Don't be so focused on getting to your next that you miss out on the great lessons or connections you're able to make where you currently are. Finally, if you have feelings of doubt, like I did, explore them. Don't be afraid. They could lead you to your destiny and your God-given purpose.

I'm still working on figuring out what my God-given purpose in life is, but I have more comfort in knowing it won't be found by living "inside the box." Like Thasunda Duckett, one of my favorite female powerhouse CEOs, once said, "Live your life like a diversified portfolio." There's no limit to what we can do or accomplish.

About Uniqua Quillins

Uniqua Quillins is a native of Beloit, Wisconsin, and a 2016 graduate of North Carolina Agricultural and Technical State University. She obtained her Bachelor's degree in Journalism and Mass Communication.

Today, Uniqua is a news producer for WSOC-TV in Charlotte, North Carolina – following her passion of telling stories that serve and impact the local community. She's one of the best-selling authors of The HBCU Experience: The North Carolina A&T State University 2nd Edition.

Uniqua is also a member of Delta Sigma Theta Sorority, Incorporated. In her free time, she loves to bowl, golf, travel and create lasting memories.

At an early age, Uniqua's family instilled in her that all things are possible through Christ. Her favorite scripture is Galatians 6:9 – "So let's not get tired of doing what is good. At just the right time we will reap a harvest of blessing if we do not give up."

The Rise of a Queen

Whitney M. Gamble

From the time I was told I was adopted at the adored age of six, I had quite the sense of "self." My parents told me I was adopted with a book titled "Adoption is for Always." I understood fully what it meant. I had a mother who birthed me alongside my birth father. But they were my parents. That's why I was a darker shade of brown than they are. I grew up during the era of rappers who constantly told us through blasting twelve-inch subwoofers, "Light skin's the right skin."

My image of beauty growing up did not look like me. It looked like my beautiful fair- skinned mother, light-skinned cousins, and fair-skinned friends. The video models we saw back then were never darker than a brown paper bag, until Sean Paul dropped "I'm Still in Love with You". This gave dark-skinned girls a new point of view on beauty in one of the world's richest shades. I always had what may have been considered lofty and grandiose dreams of being a dancer, singer, actress and hair stylist. I loved the stage. At age six, I even pushed someone off of it for messing up in her steps. Becky needed to tighten up. But I never quite knew how I, this little Black girl who was born and adopted in Omaha, Nebraska, who loved to entertain and command the stage, would ever make it to the big screen in Hollywood from Savannah, Georgia.

Growing up in Savannah was beautiful. But it was full of ugly reminders of this country's not-so-distant past, which is marred with slavery and institutionalized racism. I grew up about forty-five minutes from where Ahmaud Arbery was murdered. Visiting buildings that the slaves built on field trips, learning about how badly the South lost in the war in which they championed for slavery, and with every trip to visit family in other states, the cotton fields served as reminders that we were not welcome, nor even considered human beings, at one point in time. It was scary to be Black at times in Social Studies readings about this country's past.

I was grateful to have successful Black parents who truly built me up in every way. My dad always encouraged me to speak my mind and defend myself. My mom taught me how to do it with class. She is the epitome of class, and her little apple had to fall from that same tree. I was never allowed to speak with too much of a "Southern twang" as it's called because, as an educator and principal raised in the Midwest, my mom wasn't having that. Little did I know how much her not allowing me to be a total product of my environment would come in handy for me later in life.

Although racism is tough to deal with, shadeism is an even tougher experience because you experience it from your own. When you grow up thinking lighter and/or whiter is better, and you don't see the examples we have today, like Michelle Obama, on TV and in magazines, it paints a different picture of what the word "beautiful" means to a little Black girl. I spent time hiding under the blankets at the beach simply because I thought getting darker in the sun would make me ugly. My parents couldn't understand it then. But, to me, sitting in the sun all day would take me farther away from looking like them.

It was hard to feel like I could be pretty being dark-skinned, especially when I went through my ugly duckling stage with braces and couldn't smile pretty for a single yearbook photo. Even hearing the infamous backhanded compliment of, "You're pretty for a dark-skinned girl" felt like they were saying, "Well, you're pretty. But you still are at a disadvantage."

So, imagine how insane I thought my eight-year-old sister sounded when she suggested I do a pageant. This wasn't a regular pageant. It was The National American Miss Teen Georgia pageant, to be exact. I was about to be a senior in high school. Somehow, she and two of my friends who were entering the pageant as well thought it would be a great idea for me to enter, too. I literally threw the application in the trash. I had all the self-doubt in the world. Again, I was asking myself, "How could I, a Black girl from Savannah, accomplish this?"

After a day or so, I saw the application in the trash, unscathed.

I got it out. My little sister Taylor said, "You should do it! You could win!" I rolled my eyes and told her that she sounded crazy. In hindsight, it's crazy how much more my sister believed in me than I believed in myself. After calling relatives and going door to door in my middle class 3% Black neighborhood, I raised enough money for entry fees. I qualified with good grades and community service as a finalist to compete in the 2006 National American Miss Teen Georgia pageant, without ever asking my parents' permission.

That convo of, "I've gotta get to Atlanta for these dates" didn't go over too well. Nor did the fact that my prepared speech was garbage when my parents asked to hear it. I still had a stain on my dress from prom, even though it had just been picked up from the cleaners on the way to Atlanta.

To enter the pageant world uncoached is common. To enter the pageant world uncoached and win a national pageant is unheard of, especially as a Black woman. The odds were beyond stacked against me in the eyes of many, including my own. I had never been judged on looks for anything in life. Dark-skinned girls got no love. So, if anything, this pageant was going to be something to remember with my friends. Boy, was I right about that. After days of public speaking, the formal dress competition, the talent competition, and interviews, it was time to find out who would take the crown.

I'll never forget hours before the Top 10 finalists were announced. I was using the bathroom and heard news that stung. It was a sharp knife in the gut reminder of where I was. A woman and her daughter came in and said, "You know who is going to win queen this year. She was the runner up last year and you know how this goes. The runner up has always won the next year." Her daughter commented on a Black girl she thought was doing really well.

Her mom cut her off and said, "Well, you know they'll never win."

I couldn't believe my ears. If there was ever a moment when I wanted to give up that weekend, it was that one. It was clearly rigged. *Why even try? They're not going to choose a Black girl for this.* That self- doubt is truly the devil. Right after over-hearing that, and feeling somewhat defeated, we had our final interviews with an all-white panel of judges. I literally had to decide down to the moment if I would be real or give them *pageant girl* answers.

The most important question I was asked was, "Why are you doing this?" It was an easy answer. I was a cheerleading coach at the time to girls aged five to eight. It was important to show them, especially the little Black girls, that they could accomplish any dream if they worked hard at their passions and gifts. It was important for them to see me trying something I had never done, and hopefully winning. It was important for them to see me putting my best foot forward, despite the odds.

The moment arrived. In top three were two Black girls. One was from Africa with an accent and even richer and darker skin than mine. She was the runner up. I, this little adopted Black girl from Savannah, was officially crowned as queen. My question had finally been answered...This Queen now had a way to pursue those once impossible, lofty, and grandiose dreams...

About Whitney M. Gamble

Hailing from the coastal city of Savannah, this Georgia Peach took her dreams and talents to the West Coast at 18 after winning her first pageant and becoming National American Miss Teen Georgia in 2006. From starring on the big screen alongside Danny Glover and Laz Alonso to moving behind a lens and launching her own photography company, she is a true creative that loves to capture and entertain, and has had her share of adversity in life and the industry...which is why her testimony is one for the ages.

Fraud

Zenobia McCoy

It was a real punch in the gut. My heart was leaping out of my chest every time eyes were on me. Was I a fraud? There were times I felt like an imposter ... like I had absolutely no right to be there. Or my getting there was sheer luck. But "luck" … that word always toyed with me because I adamantly do not believe in coincidences or luck. Everything is rooted in intent, even when we only see what sprouts. But there I was, questioning everything and doubting my opportunity.

It was the first time that quitting was served to me on a decorated platter, and I was ready to feast. I was already rejected from two doctoral programs. Why would this one be any different? I filled out an entire application with all supplements, only to let it sit for seven months. All I had to do was press "submit" and I couldn't. I couldn't bring myself to press a button. Clicking "submit" opened feelings of being inadequate and mediocre. It was also the possible door for yet another rejection notice.

Now, I've experienced rejection before. But, for some reason, being rejected from a doctoral program shook my confidence. It made me question everything I grew up knowing.

Well, it got a little deeper for me. I couldn't express how I felt. I felt as if people just wouldn't understand. My story doesn't start with, "I made it despite all my doubters" or the infamous "Shout out to all my haters." From the beginning, I had a tribe of supporters, and the village only strengthened as I got older. I couldn't go to people with my doubts because it would result in being suffocated with words of encouragement and unintentionally dismissing my cry. So, I took a seven-month pause. The expectations of others, and the belief in my ability to achieve, went without question. I was placed on the esteemed pedestal of success. Yet, I literally was drowning in uncertainty.

I began to feel guilty and selfish. Others would love the overflow of support. It may be the very thing that gets them to the next level. Here I was trying to silence everything for just a second because "people wouldn't understand." Or trying to figure out why I didn't understand.

One Wednesday evening, my mother asked, "Nobi, did you submit your application yet?"

I simply responded, "No. Not yet."

She briefly recalled a story she had heard on the gospel station 1190 am about stepping out on faith. She didn't go deep into it. She didn't even pry as to why I was waiting, but that was different, too. One thing about my mother, she's going to ask what she wants to know. But the conversation stopped right there and an internal one surfaced. That question led me back to a statement that was made to me a few years back.

I was reminded that people are assigned to me and my purpose. So, my delay in fully stepping into my purpose was holding others from achieving their purpose. Talk about loaded and honestly terrifying. But those were the two thoughts that rattled in my mind for the rest of the evening.

Two weeks later, on Tuesday, January 30, 2018 at 8:48 p.m., I submitted my application to pursue my Ed.D. in Multicultural and Urban Education.

From there, I was selected to interview on March 29, 2018 with the admissions board. I was required to take a writing exam. Now the doubt really started to take full control. I took the day off to prepare my mind. Literally, everything that could have gone wrong went wrong. I left my house two hours early, only to be stuck in traffic and show up at the wrong address. With thirty minutes to get to the correct building, I panicked. All I wanted to do was cry, but I didn't have time. I ran to the building in heels (I'm far from a runner and I don't wear heels), completely out of breath, and followed the signs to the room. When I got to the door, a woman came out and said, "Sorry for keeping you waiting. We are wrapping up. Can you give us ten minutes?"

I agreed, but I really wanted to have a praise break! At that moment, I knew God ain't play about me!

My time finally came, and the interview felt more like a conversation. There were questions exchanged on both sides. At the end, one of the interviewers said, "Whatever happens, never stop pursuing what you're doing. Your passion took over the interview. You are the start for a lot of people."

At this point, I just knew God was showing out.

Fast forward to April 20, 2018 at 4:37 p.m. I received an email that read the following:

Dear Zenobia:

Congratulations! You have been accepted into the doctoral program in Learning and Teaching. You'll receive a formal letter with details sometime next week.

Enjoy the weekend.

A multitude of emotions completely took over my body. All I could do was say, "Thank you!" continuously.

Classes were set to begin in the summer. On the first day of class, I felt like an imposter. *Would I know what to say? Would I have any previous knowledge about the topics? Was there anything I could possibly contribute to the conversations?*

I walked in class. I was not only the youngest one in the class, but the only Black person in the class. I felt a wealth of pressure. The professor posed questions, and I only answered them internally. Then, I grew upset when someone said the same thing because I was continuing to doubt myself.

In another class, a professor asked me questions about my academic background. He asked if I had attended private school or if I was in a gifted and talented program. I had not. I was not. He was astonished that I was a product of NYC Department of Education, who attended

North Carolina A&T State University, an HBCU for undergrad. He was also astonished by the fact that I'd attended an online school, Southern New Hampshire University, for my master's degree. Now, here I was at Hofstra, admitted into a program that only selects eleven applicants. As a matter of fact, there were only eight people selected that year. His astonishment bothered me. It was that kind of mindset that I'm always trying to diminish within the education system.

That insulting interaction, which I'm sure was supposed to be a commendable moment, made me remember exactly who I was. Though still nervous and doubtful, I had to present myself in the way my village always saw me. That professor viewed me as a lot of people in the world view my students: as token stories. Achievement for Black and brown students shouldn't be barrier breaking. It should be the norm! That has always been my focus as an educator. I repeatedly tell my students to block out the doubt and tackle every situation like it's already theirs. I tell them to create an opportunity where it's not presented and be true to themselves throughout the entire process, even when it's not popular. Here I was, being hypocritical! I really had to remind myself just who I was. I had leaned even more on my community of supporters and found an outlet to express myself when doubt tried to rear its ugly head. I had to remind myself that I belonged anywhere and everywhere God granted me the opportunity to be.

Today, I'm two classes away from completing my degree. I've been recommended for opportunities and offered opportunities along the way. I will be graduating with my doctorate. But I will also be leaving with the credentials to be a superintendent and principal. To think, I thought I didn't belong or that I wouldn't measure up. This journey is far from over, but it's taught me how even the slightest doubt can take over and hinder opportunities. Despite what the odds may be, continue to move forward in pursuit of your desires. Even when the next step isn't clear, take it anyway and learn as you go. Everything is truly intentional. It aligns, even if you don't discover the connection until later. What you are called to do is bigger than any doubt, insecurity or life's obstacles.

About Zenobia McCoy

Zenobia E. McCoy is a passion enthusiast who truly believes that all visions are intentional and meant to come to fruition. She refuses to believe in a world where there are indefinite limitations, for there is always a way.

Zenobia was born and raised in Brooklyn, New York. She is an educator within the New York City Department of Education. Zenobia is currently earning her Ed.D degree in Multicultural/ Urban Education from Hofstra University. Prior to attending Hofstra, she earned an M.A. degree (2017) in English from Southern New Hampshire University, and a B.S. degree (2013) in Secondary English Education from North Carolina Agricultural and Technical State University.

Since childhood, Zenobia has always been an advocate for equitable education and resources in underserved communities. Her lifelong pursuit focuses on closing the opportunity gap despite the socio-economic statuses of communities.

Made in United States
North Haven, CT
21 November 2021